Table of Contents

Introduction 3
Using this book 8
YPO Forum (existing YPO Forum members may skip this bit) 10
The Forum participants 13
The listener's mindset. 15
    Be patient. 18
    Come wearing a white belt. 25
    Curiosity did not kill the cat, judgment did. 28
    To advise or not to advise, that is the question. 34
    It's Netflix time. 41
    Go raw, process less. 46
    Go with the flow and be positive. 51
    Forget Waze, ask for directions. 56
    Be mindful of the potential pitfalls of empathy. 59
    Be Creative. 64
The sharer 70
    Why bother? 73
    What do we mean by deep sharing? 79
        Introducing the ±5% sharing 79
        A deeper look into ±5% sharing 81
        I'm still grappling with the opportunity or challenge to present to my Forum. 83
    The Sharer Mindset 86
About the Author 93
Disclaimer 95
Acknowledgements 97

© Ahal Besorai 2023

Exercise Bank 99
  Be patient. 99
  Come wearing a white belt. 104
  Curiosity in, judgement out 108
  To advise or not to advise 117
  Be positive. 121
  It's Netflix time. 126
  Go raw, process less. 130
  Be creative. 139
  Openness 150
  Curiosity 163
  Authenticity 171
  Respect 180
  Action-oriented 186

© Ahal Besorai 2023

Introduction

"With the right mindset, we can't lose—we either practice what we've learned, or we learn what we need to practice."

– Noura

Your life is only as good as your mindset and so is your Forum experience.

YPO is about creating monumental impact for one's business and life. Forum is at the heart of that endeavour, as the most profound influence one can encounter arises from engaging with likeminded peers.

Forum members, on the whole, aspire to forge deeper connections, delve into meaningful discussions, and establish a sacred space where authenticity reigns, free from the need for self-censorship or pretence. Stepping out of a Forum meeting with an undeniable sense of purpose, having embraced one's true calling, fostered genuine friendships, and bathed in the liberating flow of love, elevates the Forum experience into the realm of pure magic.

However, the "Forum magic" hardly ever occurs by itself. It requires, on top of the success principles, best practices, and protocols, for Forum members to employ the right mindset so

© Ahal Besorai 2023

that their Forum morphs into the fertile ground on which seeds of personal growth are planted and nurtured.

The value added that you gain, and can impart to your Forum colleagues, will only come in proportion to your ability to adopt an effective Forum participant's mindset. Not all Forum members are great participants. Some aren't effective at all, while others are simply amazing. My assumption is that you want to be a great Forum participant. This is a wonderful goal and one that pretty much anyone who is willing to learn, grow, and persevere can achieve.

I joined my first Forum some 20 years ago. But I did not start off as an effective participant. I started as a terrible one. I made many mistakes, and I was a bit stubborn in thinking that whatever I did was right and however I participated was what Effective Participation must be.

My journey toward becoming an effective participant took me through a lot of changes and required a lot of development. The most significant aspect of my growth was my transformation from participation at the skill level to being a participant at the deeper level of how I think.

As you advance towards your aim of becoming an effective Forum participant, allow me to provide some guidance: engaging actively in the Forum is commendable, but the high leverage shift isn't in your doing – it's in your thinking. You might even say it's in your being.

Too many times I have seen new (and even seasoned) Forum participants get in the way, do it wrong, and just make a mess of the Forum decorum. More times than not they do it wrong because they think wrong. When working with these Forums, they most often want to know what to do differently - how to listen, how to exercise self-curiosity, how to apply best practices and protocols, how to ask provoking questions, how to do updates, how to deal with lack of commitment and so forth.

These are all good things, but those are techniques. And the right techniques in the wrong hands will still produce the wrong result. As a Forum participant what you need most isn't simply to master the techniques (although that will doubtlessly enhance the Forum experience), but to master the way you think. When you think like an effective Forum participant, the techniques just click, the conversation flows smoothly, and you bring and gain tremendous value. Thinking like an effective Forum participant requires not just a change in what you do, but also a change in who you are. When that deep level change occurs, the proper techniques and skills and protocols come naturally and fluidly.

© Ahal Besorai 2023

My transformation to become an effective participant hinged on a huge change in my thinking. In this book my hope is to help you experience a similar change. Whether you are an existing Forum member or considering joining one, this book is designed to help you understand the effective Forum participant mindset, to notice your mindset and that of your Forum colleagues and to actually inhabit that mindset so that it becomes a part of who you are, not just something you do.

"But my Forum is doing just fine, why should I bother with all this mindset stuff?" I sort of hear you wonder. "Really, why bother?"

This is a fair question, and my answer is simple - if 'doing just fine' is good enough for you, then you have a point. However, if your pursuit of excellence extends to your Forum participation, and 'doing just fine' is falling short of that, then making the effort to improve the way you participate in Forum, might not be such a cumbersome proposition.

"And above all, watch with glittering eyes the whole world around you because the greatest secrets are always hidden in the most unlikely places. Those who don't believe in magic will never find it."

— Roald Dahl

© Ahal Besorai 2023

So, together, let's embark on a journey to create magic. Take the step forward, embrace the possibilities, and let the enchantment unfold.

© Ahal Besorai 2023

Using this book

"One must always be careful of books," said Tessa, "and what is inside them, for words have the power to change us."

— Cassandra Clare, Clockwork Angel

I'm aware that changing mindsets is a formidable task, requiring courage to venture into uncharted territory. It also necessitates resilience, as initial changes may feel uncomfortable and yield uncertain results.

Acknowledging these challenges, to effectively leverage the teachings in this book, my suggestion is to start with small steps and gradually build upon them. Begin by examining the different mindsets presented below and assess their perceived levels of difficulty for you personally. Rank them in order of difficulty, starting with the mindset that appears easiest to adopt and practice it during your next Forum meeting. Take note of how it feels, identify any challenges you face, and make necessary adjustments to your behavior and approach.

As you become more comfortable with the initial mindset and witness the positive impact it has, progress to the next mindset on your list. Continuously iterate this process, working through each mindset and integrating them into your Forum participation. Over time, the aim is for these mindsets

© Ahal Besorai 2023

to become second nature and significantly enhance the effectiveness of your Forum engagements.

Similarly, the entire Forum can collectively undertake this approach, with each member striving to improve their individual attitude—one mindset at a time. This 'doing it together' approach will foster mutual understanding and support, as members learn from each other's personal struggles with specific mindsets, offering assistance in areas where some may find it easier than others.

At the end of the book, I included exercises to serve as valuable tools to reinforce your learnings and further develop your Forum mindset. They are specifically designed to help you (and the Forum) practice and master the required mindsets discussed throughout the book.

By actively engaging with these exercises, you can further internalise the principles and concepts introduced in the text. The exercises provide practical scenarios and prompts that encourage you to apply the mindsets in real-life situations, both within and outside of the Forum.

© Ahal Besorai 2023

YPO Forum (existing YPO Forum members may skip this bit)

The YPO Forum, established by members of the Northern California Chapter in 1975, fulfils a crucial need for YPO members. YPO leaders often feel isolated at the pinnacle of their organisations, lacking an authentic outlet to address their challenges and opportunities, be they business-related, family-related, or personal in nature.

Originally conceived to provide a genuine venue for YPO members to unpack their issues, the Forum has grown into a global phenomenon with over 4,100 active Forums worldwide. It has become an integral part of YPO's cultural fabric, with its unique language permeating the organisation's global vocabulary. In fact, the Forum is considered the primary reason why new members join YPO, as it offers unparalleled value and benefits.

However, the impact of the Forum extends far beyond the business arena. Many members attest that participation in Forum has not only enhanced their leadership skills, but has also transformed them into better parents, spouses, partners, and overall, better human beings. Alongside the traditional member Forums, various other Forum types are available,

© Ahal Besorai 2023

such as spouse Forums, microForums, and network Forums, catering to diverse needs and interests.

A Forum comprises a close-knit group of eight to ten peers who regularly convene in an environment characterised by trust, confidentiality, and openness. It provides a safe haven where participants can share and discuss their professional and personal experiences, ensuring ongoing support and valuable insights.

What sets YPO Forums apart is their unique structure. Unlike business-oriented personal advisory groups facilitated by paid professionals, YPO Forums are entirely peer-moderated. The moderator, chosen by the members themselves, undergoes specialised training through the Forum Moderator & Leadership Development workshop. While the moderator plays a crucial role, the responsibility for effective meetings and maintaining the Forum's health lies with all members, highlighting the collective commitment to fostering a thriving Forum community.

It's important to clarify what the Forum isn't. It's not a fix-it group, social club, therapy session, advice-giving platform, judgmental space, or a networking organisation. The essence of the Forum lies in creating a trusted space where peers can

© Ahal Besorai 2023

engage in meaningful, supportive discussions without ulterior motives or conflicting interests.

While the primary focus is on the YPO Forum's format, it's worth noting that this format and the mindsets discussed in this book, with perhaps a few slight modifications, can be adapted to other types of Forums and organisations wanting to benefit from the growth potential, transformation, and personal development that Forum has to offer. A family Forum or business Forum are two very good examples. Although the dynamics in these would be different to those in a YPO Forum, and as noted, adaptations might be required, there are many successful experiences that demonstrate the benefits of such Forums for their participants.

All in all, the methodologies and techniques explored in this book can be valuable resources for anyone seeking personal growth and self-development, in or outside a Forum.

© Ahal Besorai 2023

The Forum participants

"She just smiled, said that she loved books more than anything, and started telling him excitedly what each of the ones in her lap was about. And Ove realised that he wanted to hear her talking about the things she loved for the rest of his life."

— Fredrik Backman, A Man Called Ove

In the Forum, participants assume two distinct roles: listeners and sharers.

As listeners, individuals actively engage when their Forum peers, share experiences, participate in self-discovery exercises, provide updates, or explore a particular topic. On the other hand, as sharers, participants contribute by sharing their own challenges and opportunities, seeking insights and guidance from their Forum colleagues.

Regrettably, on occasion, listeners, with good intentions, may inadvertently prioritise assisting their peers in achieving what they want, rather than what they truly need. Similarly, sharers sometimes explore non-Forum issues that fall outside the essential 5% (matters that could be better suited for casual conversations with friends). There are also times when participants may feel pressured to share challenges without knowing how to approach it effectively, or may lack confidence in expressing emotions and being vulnerable.

The primary objective of this book is to empower you to adopt the right mindset that maximises the benefits of your Forum experience. Whether participating as listener - seeking to be helpful - or unpacking your own challenges as sharer: each role demands a distinct mindset. My hope is that this book be used as a Forum companion assisting you and your Forum to create Forum Magic by adopting the right mindset to bring with you to your next Forum meeting.

© Ahal Besorai 2023

The listener's mindset.

"We possess two ears and only one mouth with a purpose: to encourage us to listen twice as much as we speak."

– Unknown

A good listener explains.

An excellent listener demonstrates.

A great listener inspires.

A masterful listener creates the space for miracles to occur. (And then their colleagues think they did it themselves!)

A mindset is a set of beliefs that shape how you make sense of the world and yourself. It influences how you think, feel, and behave in any given situation. It means that what you believe about yourself impacts your success or failure.

According to Stanford psychologist Carol Dweck, your beliefs play a pivotal role in what you want and whether you achieve it. Dweck has found that it's your mindset that plays a significant role in determining achievement and success.

Mindsets can influence how people behave in a wide range of situations in life. For example, as people encounter different situations, their mind triggers a specific mindset that then directly impacts their behaviour in that situation.

Let's look the number 8549176320. It's quite special. Can you guess what is unique about it?

Problem-solving requires a change in your attitude — almost a new mindset. It draws out the unconscious strategies you use for dealing with challenges.

The answer is that this sequence of numbers has all the digits arranged in alphabetical order. Didn't expect that, did you?

You and your Forum colleagues have consistent patterns of thinking and even consistent thoughts. Your mindset defines your beliefs, and your compulsions. Increase your Forum colleagues' awareness and you'll increase their power and impact over their life.

Too often we try to address strategic problems with tactical solutions, wondering why we fail in the long run.

If we don't help ourselves and our Forum colleagues to address these challenges at their deepest level, it's inevitable that the same issues will keep recurring.

In this part of the book, I introduce the mindsets that you need to become an effective Forum listener. My hope is to help you

© Ahal Besorai 2023

experience the change in order to transform yourself into an effective listener, so in your next Forum meeting, you try not only to be a better listener of others, but also of yourself. Where you don't just focus on the information, but rather focus on the feeling and able to stay 'in' the feeling. Not trying to fix it or push it away. Just letting it be there and then simply look to understand why it's there.

Listening well is not simply hearing the words being said, it's also feeling the emotions being felt. People usually don't want solutions as much as they just want to be understood.

© Ahal Besorai 2023

Be patient.

"Patience is a virtue, and I'm learning patience. It's a tough lesson."

— Elon Musk

In a Forum, we come together as individuals from diverse backgrounds, upbringings, cultures, and industries. What may be effortless for one person could be immensely challenging for another. It's common to encounter members who take longer to open up and share on a deeper level, as some of you may already have experienced in previous Forum interactions.

The difficulty lies in the vulnerability required to be open and honest. It necessitates stepping outside our comfort zones and taking risks by sharing our innermost thoughts, emotions, and experiences with others. Often, in Forum, we observe and follow the cues of the least open and vulnerable participant, as it feels safer to stay within the confines of our comfort zones.

However, by choosing to remain guarded and risk-averse in our Forum discussions, we miss out on the true potential of the experience.

My strong belief of the necessity for patience in Forum and in particular patience with members who struggle to share

© Ahal Besorai 2023

deeply, stems from my own journey as the 'tin soldier' (that childhood and early adulthood created) who has now been melted, by the power of vulnerability, kindness, tenderness, and deep sharing, into something different; softer, more accepting and caring. This process has been fostered to a large part by my Forum friends and YPO. It's the patience employed by these Forum friends that ultimately helped me to cross that Rubicon. And they employed a patient mindset (well, most of the time) despite their frustration at my rigidity, lack of ability to be vulnerable and the numerous masks I had on. Don't get me wrong, I tried especially hard to be open and vulnerable, I just lacked the tools, the ability to reach that soft and raw inner core. Any attempt to do so was painful and frankly very scary.

Here are some of difficulties I faced trying to be more vulnerable, remove the masks, be more authentic and sharing more deeply: -

1. **Fear of judgment**: Many people hesitate to be vulnerable because they fear being judged or criticised by others. They worry about how their colleagues might perceive their thoughts, feelings, or personal experiences. This fear can lead to a reluctance to share openly.

© Ahal Besorai 2023

2. **Past negative experiences**: Previous experiences of rejection, betrayal, or mistreatment can make it difficult for individuals to trust others and open up. They may carry emotional baggage from these experiences, causing them to be more guarded and protective of their vulnerabilities.

3. **Cultural or societal norms**: Cultural or societal norms can play a significant role in shaping individuals' behavior and attitudes towards vulnerability. In some cultures, expressing emotions or personal struggles may be considered inappropriate or weak, leading individuals to avoid sharing their true thoughts and feelings.

4. **Self-preservation instincts**: Vulnerability requires individuals to expose their true selves, which can make them feel vulnerable to potential harm or exploitation. Some people may have developed self-preservation mechanisms that make it challenging for them to let their guard down and be vulnerable with others.

5. **Lack of trust**: Building trust is crucial for individuals to feel comfortable opening up. If there is a lack of trust within the work environment, whether due to past experiences or a competitive atmosphere, colleagues

© Ahal Besorai 2023

may be hesitant to share their vulnerabilities for fear of it being used against them.

6. **Perceived professional image**: Colleagues may feel the need to maintain a professional image and worry that being vulnerable could be seen as a sign of weakness. They may fear that showing their vulnerabilities could impact how they are perceived by their peers or superiors, affecting their career prospects or opportunities.

Understanding these challenges (which by the way aren't exclusive to me), helps develop greater empathy and patience towards your Forum colleagues who struggle with opening up and being vulnerable. Some members find it extremely easy to wear their heart on their sleeve and some would find it hard to acknowledge that they have one at all (heart that is). It's the willingness to be patient and give members the time and space they need that ultimately fosters an atmosphere of understanding, empathy, and trust that encourages colleagues to feel safe and comfortable sharing their thoughts, emotions, and personal experiences.

Patience also plays a role in taming the expectation you may have of your young Forum. In the early stages of a Forum, it's common to feel that the Forum is performing less than expected. This might be because you hear members of more mature Forums share how valuable the experience is for them and you somehow feel your Forum does not perform to the same level. Additionally, the amount of information and protocol that needs to be taken in and followed on top of the need to be vulnerable and in touch with one's emotions (which might be a new experience), makes the Forum practice feel technical and head-based rather than emotional and heart-based. You will also probably lose a few members and integrate new ones, have to firm the meaning of commitment and vulnerability, and even question your own commitment to something that was sold to you as the best experience in YPO. That is OK. It takes 2-4 years on average for a Forum to get to an effective performing state, for members to jell together and for a sense of flow and rhythm to emerge. So just be patient, the magic will happen.

For those who are less patient and want a highly effective Forum earlier, some of the ways which I found helpful to shorten the process are: -

1. For all Forum members to agree to attend moderator training within 12 months of joining the Forum (this can be integrated into the Forum norms). And thereafter every 2 years.

© Ahal Besorai 2023

2. Allowing members who cannot fully commit to graciously leave the Forum. See "The limits of patience" below.

3. To appoint a process officer to ensure members follow the various protocols and norms and to allocate time at the end of each meeting for that officer to air his/her findings. It's helpful if the process officer possesses the tendencies of a Sergeant Major and isn't shy or subdued by talking to people and making sure they toe the line.

4. To have a retreat and/or supercharge (preferably externally facilitated) once a year.

The limits of Patience

As busy individuals seeking a meaningful return on our time investment, we understand the importance of creating a Forum environment where genuine sharing and authentic connections thrive. When a Forum member{s} is unable or unwilling to commit to this level of openness and vulnerability, it can hinder the Forum's potential to achieve the transformative and magical experience that other members expect.

If it becomes evident that someone's lack of commitment is impeding the Forum's progress and preventing the desired

© Ahal Besorai 2023

level of engagement, then thoughtful action might be necessary.

Taking action does not necessarily mean expelling someone from the Forum immediately. Instead, it could involve an off Forum one-on-one meeting, endeavouring to understand the reasons behind their inability to share more deeply and display vulnerability.

However, if, after concerted efforts and time, it becomes clear that an individual's unwillingness to engage authentically is persisting, then the Forum may need to consider more substantial actions. This could involve having a compassionate and respectful conversation about whether the Forum is the right fit for them or, in rare cases, a mutual understanding that they may need to step aside to allow others to fully participate.

A word of advice: before resorting to cutting the rope, take the time to explore all possible ways to untie the knot.

© Ahal Besorai 2023

Come wearing a white belt.

"I don't know." That was typical Sajaki; like all the genuinely clever people Sylveste had met he knew better than to feign understanding where none existed."

— Alastair Reynolds, Revelation Space

Since you were a young child, you were rewarded for being smart; and being smart has always been considered better than being stupid. As a CEO or leader, the smart > dumb equation has just been further reinforced. However, in a Forum setting, being too smart is a hinderance.

When you consider that the highest value that you bring to your Forum colleagues is your intellect, your brilliance, your amazing problem-solving abilities as demonstrated by the black belt around your kimono, you get in the way. That is because effective Forum participation is about drawing on the intellect, brilliance, amazing problem-solving ability, and creativity of your fellow Forum members.

That is why I propose the idea of attending Forum meetings metaphorically wearing a white belt – stop trying to solve the explorer's challenges, stop trying to figure it all out. I know, it's mightily difficult to stop these seemingly smart activities. It's difficult to take off the black belt we acquired through so

© Ahal Besorai 2023

much fixing and solving, as well as being capable, and decisive, and determined etc, etc etc, ultimately these are the skills that got us here in the first place. But we should try.

On the one hand, we humans are wired for connection; it's in our DNA to find safe, meaningful connections with others in all types of relationships. In a Forum, this ability to connect plays a crucial role. However, on the other hand our human brain is also an incredible pattern-matching machine. When we see something new, we try to connect it to something familiar, something we have already encountered, something for which we have a category and maybe even a solution. And we, YPOers, have bags and bags of familiar previous encounters and solutions. But our efficient pattern-machine ability is a detriment when it's coming to Forum because our Forum colleagues' brains are also effective pattern-solving machines and our job is to get their brains working, not just show off how well ours does.

Arriving with a white belt is like instructing our brain to temporarily alter its usual functioning. We do this because our Forum brain needs to operate differently from our typical CEO brain. The Forum brain works not to solve, but to facilitate the problem-solving abilities of our Forum colleagues. Our Forum brain should not preoccupy itself with

© Ahal Besorai 2023

thinking multiple steps ahead; instead, it should strive to be with the person sharing in the present moment as they think and share.

Curiosity did not kill the cat, judgment did.

"The mind is not a vessel to be filled, but a fire to be kindled."

— Plutarch

Curiosity is the expression of the urge to learn and acquire facts and knowledge. It widens the mind and opens it to different opinions, different lifestyles and different topics. In Forum, being curious is important because it means that we're willing to inhabit a space of not knowing. We ask the best questions and share the most relevant experiences and invite other Forum members to think best when we're curious.

Curiosity in Forum isn't about satiating our gossip-like tendencies; like we sometimes do when flicking through the pages of Hello Magazine or Vanity Fair. The curiosity we display isn't about us, but about what is shared. That is to say, we should exhibit curiosity which is positive and focused on the sharer. Something like – "that is interesting, I wonder where this is going?".

The enemy of curiosity is judgement. A judging attitude says, "I know what this is." As humans, we're naturally wired to draw conclusions from our life experiences at face value. Perhaps you heard that someone declared bankruptcy and you immediately assume that they are irresponsible with money, without considering unforeseen circumstances or financial hardships they may have faced. Or seeing a person with a visible tattoo makes you assume they are rebellious or irresponsible. Well, that is your judgmental brain talking.

But no matter how instinctive judgment is for us, making the effort to go against it and to practice non-judgment can change our lives for the better. By being non-judgmental, we become more compassionate and accepting of ourselves and others.

It's not that our judgments are always negative, as in "I know what this is, and it's bad." However, judging something as positive can be just as detrimental to open sharing because judging shuts down the learning process. Curiosity, on the other hand, opens up the sharing process.

Imagine that a Forum member brings as his issue that his son has decided not to go to college/university to pursue a degree. Looking at this with a judgmental mindset, you might say "Oh, that is bad, I bet that is upsetting", and then ask, "what can you do to change his mind?". Employing a curious mindset would result in "I wonder what my Forum member thinks and feels about that", and then asking, "what do you think of that? Or think back to when he first told you he was dropping out, what was your first thought?" …How are you thinking about it now?" The judgement mindset assumes

© Ahal Besorai 2023

what the issue is and races to tackle it; meanwhile, the curious mindset invites the member to explore what is going on, to expand his/her understanding of the situation, and creates new awareness before rushing into action.

Sometimes simply the language you use can come across as judgmental. Look at questions beginning with *Why*. While *Why* is considered an open-ended question, it does not elicit powerful and fresh answers. Why questions actually create defensive and scripted responses.

Think about times when someone asked you questions like these and what it made you feel:

- Why did you do this?
- Why do you charge so much?
- Why do you think like that?

To avoid coming across as being judgmental, try to reframe the Why questions as the below demonstrates.

- Why did you do this? becomes - how did this happen?
- Why do you charge so much? becomes - how was this pricing structure decided?
- Why do you think like that? Becomes - how is it that you learned that? or how did you come to that understanding?

© Ahal Besorai 2023

Dropping the *Why* from our questions requires us to think differently. We need to translate our Why questions into How or What questions. You will find that these simple changes in phrasing will lead to more engaged and open responses. And while it may be difficult to break this seemingly innocent and well-intentioned habit, start by becoming aware of judgement that could be perceived from the way you phrase a question to a Forum colleague.

Maintaining a curious mindset can indeed serve as a potent catalyst for promoting, facilitating, and encouraging open dialogue among colleagues in a Forum. Consider this example. Have you ever met someone who asserted she had no issues? Well, I did.

When that happened, a brief judgmental thought crossed my mind—"can a person truly have no issues?" —but I chose to embrace curiosity and delved deeper. I inquired "could you elaborate on that?" In response, she shared that, at this stage of her life, she actively shields herself from negativity, employing a methodology to diffuse potential issues before they even arise. Intrigued by her approach, my curiosity intensified, and I expressed my desire to learn more, and she obliged. "That's truly remarkable! Would you be willing to share this approach with your Forum?" I asked. "Sure" was

© Ahal Besorai 2023

her reply. At the retreat, she revealed her method for averting the emergence of issues, using a specific past problem she had faced as a discussion point. The act of vulnerability and profound sharing by this participant not only provided an opportunity for Forum members to witness a previously unseen side of her but also alleviated any judgmental perceptions that may have existed – can a person truly have no issue? By openly sharing her approach and discussing a personal problem, she demonstrated that she too grappled with challenges, despite initially claiming to have no issues. This revelation freed Forum members from the notion that she could not contribute meaningfully to deep discussions. Instead, it allowed them to appreciate her unique perspective and experiences, fostering a greater sense of inclusiveness and empathy within the Forum.

For some of us, curiosity may seem to slow things down, but in the long run it actually speeds things up. By starting slow, we invite the sharer to get to the heart of things first and to then act based on the real issue – the underlying truth. A judging mindset often goes fast at first but then gets jammed because it tends to jump in quickly, often addressing the wrong issue.

© Ahal Besorai 2023

To listen without judgment, we start by choosing to replace that judgment with authentic curiosity. Curiosity as to what is important to our Forum friend about what they are telling us; curiosity about what you might learn from what they have to say; curiosity about how connecting rather than judging might serve you both in the moment.

Choosing to not be judgmental does not equate to agreeing with someone. Not at all. You have your beliefs, opinions, and values, and they have theirs. The difference is that when you refuse to judge, you acknowledge that they have just as much right to their beliefs as you have to yours. You give them the space and the grace to be themselves with you, which is all most of us ever ask for.

Emphatic curiosity is critical, so work on remaining curious and on inviting the sharer to get curious too. When you encourage him/her to be curious, you knock them out of autopilot and compel them to get intentional about thinking through things in a fresh, new, and more helpful way.

Listening without judgment is the doorway to connection. Emphatic curiosity is the key to that door.

© Ahal Besorai 2023

To advise or not to advise, that is the question.

"I always pass on good advice. It is the only thing to do with it. It is never of any use to oneself."

— Oscar Wilde, An Ideal Husband

There is a time and place for advice. But when giving it is your default response to a Forum colleague facing difficult situations, it becomes a problem.

Giving advice is an insidious mindset — one you have been encouraged to adopt all your life. You have spent years delivering advice and getting promoted and praised for it. You are seen to be "adding value" and you have the added bonus of staying in control of the situation. Refraining from giving advice and merely asking a question, practicing self-curiosity, or sharing an experience might feel less certain about whether you are being useful, the conversation can feel slower, and you might feel like you have somewhat lost control of the conversation. However, what you have just done is called "empowering" – calling on your Forum colleagues to learn, improve and grow, rather than to just get something sorted out. It's interesting to note that when you give advice, your brain gets a dose of feel-good chemicals.

© Ahal Besorai 2023

You feel smart and accomplished, poised and helpful. The buzz is intoxicating. No wonder you are giving advice all the time.

Some of the reasons given for not giving advice.

1. **You are tackling the incorrect challenge**. Often, you are presenting solutions (whether brilliant or not) for the wrong problem. You have fallen into the trap of believing that the initial challenge mentioned is the real issue, which is rarely the case. However, because we're all eager to help and "add value," you dive in and solve the first thing that arises. We discussed this already in "Curiosity did not kill the cat, judgment did".

2. **You are presenting a subpar solution.** Suppose you managed to avoid that initial mistake and took some time to identify the real problem. Unfortunately, you are still likely to offer suggestions that aren't as good as you perceive them to be. There are various reasons for this. Firstly, you don't have the complete picture. You possess a few facts, a collection of biases, a strong dose of opinion, and a plethora of assumptions. Your brain is wired to find patterns and make connections that give you a sense of understanding, even though you may not truly comprehend the situation. Additionally, your own self-

serving bias comes into play, which is the tendency to believe that your ideas are excellent. As a result, you continue to generate flawed recommendations.

3. **You are demonstrating a lack of supportive friendship.** Even if you manage to avoid the initial two mistakes, you will come to a point where you face a decision: Do you provide a quick and correct answer? In a Forum setting, where we're meant to be equals, with no one assumed to be less experienced or less senior, why not allow others to figure things out on their own? Offering advice may expedite the process and reinforce your position within the group, but refraining from doing so can be an empowering act. It leads to increased confidence, competence, and autonomy for others.

4. **The advice received is frequently undervalued or disregarded.** One reason for this is the presence of "egocentric bias," where individuals tend to prioritise their own opinions over the perspectives of others, even when lacking expertise in a particular matter. Seekers of advice may also struggle to comprehend the reasoning behind an advisor's perspective or become so fixed in their own preconceived notions that they are unable to adjust their thinking in the light of contrary feedback. In contrast, participants in control and low-power groups ignored

© Ahal Besorai 2023

advice about half as frequently, highlighting the impact of power dynamics on advice reception and consideration.

5. **Failing to appropriately address the consequences that follow.** If you choose to provide advice, it's crucial to understand that the ultimate decision does not rest with you. Therefore, it's important not to take offense if your guidance isn't accepted entirely, as this could hinder further discussion. In reality, recipients seldom take one person's advice at face value. Instead, they often modify the advice, incorporate feedback from others, or even reject it altogether. Unfortunately, advisors often fail to recognise these responses as valuable input in an ongoing conversation. It's essential to treat these varied responses as valuable contributions and continue the dialogue rather than becoming defensive or discouraged.

6. **Guidance Centred on the Self: Overlooking the Seeker's Perspective and Constraints.** Advisers often frame their advice as "how I would respond if I were in your shoes." However, this approach is both off-putting and ineffective because it fails to consider the seeker's feelings, perception of the situation, and understanding of the available choices. Empathetic understanding and valuable recommendations arise from insights into the seeker's unique perspective.

© Ahal Besorai 2023

For the reasons above, by and large, giving advice in a Forum context is wrong. The goal isn't to avoid ever providing an answer, but it's to get better at having people find their own answers.

Furthermore, the process of seeking and giving advice within a Forum setting presents unique challenges that require careful navigation. Participants often encounter significant obstacles rooted in their inherent biases and tend to prioritise their own opinions, regardless of their actual merit.

A common pitfall arises when individuals acknowledge the value of giving less advice, and of sharing experiences and asking more questions, but deep down they believe they possess the answer to the issue being discussed. In such situations, rather than providing direct advice, they conceal their inclination by sharing experiences and posing seemingly genuine questions. Phrases like the ones below are used as veiled ways to convey their own suggestions.

"Have you thought about implementing a more structured project management approach?" (Direct advice: Suggesting the adoption of a structured project management approach.)

© Ahal Besorai 2023

"When I encountered a challenging decision, I found that seeking input from a diverse group of stakeholders provided valuable perspectives. Maybe you could consider gathering feedback from various team members or experts to make a more informed choice." (Disguised shared experience: Describing the benefit of seeking diverse input in decision-making and suggesting the same approach to the individual.)

Some would forcefully argue (with justification) that NO advice should be given in Forum, full stop. I tend to agree, not giving advice in Forum is the preferable option. However, if the urge to give advice gets the best of you, please only do so if: -

1. Advice is specifically asked for (similar to giving feedback).
2. The person seeking advice clearly identifies their blind spots, recognises when and how to ask for guidance, draws useful insights from the advice and assesses that the Forum colleagues are the right people to give such advice, and overcomes an inevitable defensiveness about their own views.
3. It's abundantly clear that the individual seeking advice has a genuine objective beyond seeking mere validation or praise. That is to say that despite their

© Ahal Besorai 2023

confidence in having solved the problem, there remains a desire to "check the box" with their Forum colleagues or choose the easier option, primarily due to a reluctance to invest the required time and effort in pursuing a superior outcome.

If, based on the above, you have decided that giving advice is acceptable, please also remember that: -

1. When giving advice always ask yourself (and share) the experience that led you to give that advice.
2. Advice is the last resort to all other forms of Forum interactions.

© Ahal Besorai 2023

It's Netflix time.

"Nose of a dog, the heart of a marine, sounds like a hero to me!"

(Talking about Max)

— Robbie Amell

As someone who has participated in, moderated, and facilitated numerous Forum meetings, supercharges and retreats, I often find myself feeling (during these meetings) as engrossed as I'm when watching my favourite action series on Netflix. Each Forum member brings their own set of challenges, opportunities, and events happening in their lives, making it incredibly fascinating when a colleague successfully unpacks such an issue.

Now, with all the fun that entails, I'm not suggesting that you become a passive observer – a couch potato - treating the Forum meeting as an opportunity to fulfil your own needs by simply watching someone else. Instead, I encourage you to approach the Forum conversation like an adventure movie, where the person sharing becomes the star — the hero who drives the action forward.

This mindset is crucial because when a colleague discusses an issue, it's easy to mistakenly assume that their intention is for us to take centre stage. Sometimes, our colleagues may be

© Ahal Besorai 2023

experiencing real pain or trouble. However, we must resist the desire to provide immediate assistance. Instead, we should think to ourselves, "This is a challenging situation. I cannot wait to see how she/he navigates through it!" That is the essence of Forum thinking. You don't want to think, "This is a tough spot. How can I help that person overcome it?" Or even worse, make their challenge your own.

Try to envision Forum meetings as an action movie on Netflix, maybe Peaky Blinders or Narcos. In these series, the hero always manages to find a way out of difficult situations because there will be another episode and hopefully another season. When I watch Narcos, I can relax and let Steve Murphy do all the work, pursuing Pablo Escobar and the Medellín Cartel, participating in high-risk raids and arrests, escaping firefights and shootouts, or navigating the treacherous world of informants and unreliable allies. I trust Boyd Holbrook (the actor) to excel at his job and get through the challenges he faces.

Applying this analogy to a Forum meeting, we should imagine the person sharing their story as the capable, committed hero who will undoubtedly overcome their challenges—it's just a matter of how.

© Ahal Besorai 2023

Now, it's important to acknowledge that as Forum participants, we do more than just sit back, munch on popcorn, and watch the sharer's journey unfold. We actively prompt, facilitate, and engage with them through self-curiosity, asking provoking questions, sharing an experience or, upon granted permission, pointing to a bind spot the sharer missed. However, we do so with the unwavering belief that they are the heroes, capable of triumphing over their obstacles. Our confidence in them and our conviction in the exploration process bring out the best in the sharer.

You might question what should be done if truly challenging and difficult situations are brought to the Forum by certain members. Could they not benefit from our "help"? And by "help," I mean our effort, intelligence, problem-solving skills, and heroics. The answer is a resounding "NO! Absolutely not." The more daunting the challenge, the more crucial it becomes to allow the sharer to take on the role of the hero.

Exceptionally tough issues challenge the sharer's thinking and create the necessary space for growth and transformation. If we mistakenly rush in to save the sharer, we deny them the opportunity to evolve, change, and ultimately save themselves.

© Ahal Besorai 2023

A word of caution, if the issue raised by a member concerns the possibility of the sharer causing harm to themselves or someone else, then the Forum context actually ends, and we move into the realm of something different where professional help might be called for.

SOS situations

When we feel that a Forum member may be a risk to him/herself and others or the issue they raised is one that needs professional help, our empathy, and the need for us to make ourselves helpful should give way to finding the proper professional solution the member needs.

SOS situations take us outside of the scope of normal Forum and the approaches to follow aren't standard Forum practices. The Forum should not get too caught up in procedures and confidentiality and act swiftly to support the member as required.

A few possible approaches: -

Buddy system - where a Forum member proactively stayed in touch with the specific member and ensured safe communication, empathetic listening and engagement.

Reporting to Family - Sharing with the family (along with the Forum/chapter officer as required) that the specific member is a danger to self/others. Remember this is one of the exceptions of confidentiality where you can share beyond the Forum if the member is suicidal or going to harm/kill someone else.

Check out the YPO CAP system (Crisis Assistance Program). This is mainly for travel crises but may include some suicide situations.

M2Mx. M2Mx confidentially connects members and spouses/partners to share guidance and advice regarding health, business and personal issues. Access to M2Mx is included in your membership and available to all members and spouses/partners. Approaching the M2Mx might be an option, but the response process is slow and might not be suitable to an immediate SOS situation.

Enabling effective professional counselling support - help the member find effective counselling/psychiatric support.

© Ahal Besorai 2023

Go raw, process less.

"I'd come to realize that all our troubles spring from our failure to use plain, clear-cut language."

— Jean-Paul Satre

This concept is a relative (a cousin perhaps) of the coming with the white belt mindset. It involves keeping your observations, experience sharing, noticing and thoughts simple and unfiltered.

Let's explore how it typically unfolds: as the person sharing their issue speaks, your mind naturally engages in a certain level of thinking. It's only natural to have thoughts, but as your thinking continues, you may find yourself generating more intricate ideas by making connections based on your own understanding. Your brain perpetually poses and answers questions, leading you to believe that you possess valuable observations or experiences to share, a noticing to offer, or a feeling or resonance to express.

Let's consider an example: imagine a colleague participating in a Forum who expresses uncertainty about how to handle the unethical behavior of one of their co-directors. As a result, they feel trapped in this predicament. While attentively listening, your brain springs into action, giving rise to a series

© Ahal Besorai 2023

of thoughts. Your thought process might unfold in the following manner: -

"I wonder what they mean by feeling 'trapped.'" "The notion of being trapped likely implies that they are hesitant to confront the issue head-on, let alone discuss it with the co-director or shareholders." "I'm intrigued by the factors that have led to this hesitation." "Perhaps they lack the courage to take appropriate action, or maybe they are concerned about safeguarding their positive image." "So, it appears that courage plays a pivotal role here. How can we support them in cultivating more courage?"

After considerable contemplation, you might eventually pose the question, "What steps can you take to gain the necessary courage?" or share a personal experience in which you felt courageous and acted on a seemingly difficult decision.

However, the crux of the problem lies in the fact that the aforementioned question or sharing is the byproduct of overthinking. A much more effective approach would involve reverting to the initial question you posed to yourself: "What do you mean by feeling 'trapped'?" Similarly, a more impactful shared experience would entail recounting a moment when you felt utterly trapped. Such basic questions or shared experiences prompt the sharer to engage in their

© Ahal Besorai 2023

own thought processing rather than relying on you to do it for them. It's about eliciting raw and fundamental questions or shared experiences, rather than overly processed ones.

Our thought processes often elude our complete control. At times, they transpire within seconds, without us even realising it. Some equate our mind (engaged in this thought process) to an internet browser - at least 18 open tabs, 3 of them are frozen, and you have no clue where the music is coming from…

The Forum mindset encourages us to train ourselves to observe our own thinking and to pause or step back from the thought process and close the "open tabs". This paves the way for unprocessed inquiries and shared experiences that invite the sharer to delve deeper.

Not knowing it all is OK! Instinctively, we often shy away from sharing something basic because we're reluctant to admit that we aren't already familiar with it. In most conversations and relationships, when someone mentions a movie, a sports game, or a technological device, we prefer to possess prior knowledge on the subject matter. We aspire to be "in the know" and avoid feeling left out. Consequently, when a colleague, in a Forum, mentions feeling trapped, a part of us hesitates to acknowledge that we don't fully grasp their intended meaning. Erroneously, we perceive asking a basic question as a request for an explanation regarding something we should already comprehend. However, that is far from the truth—basic questions and basic sharing serve as powerful invitations for the sharer to explore their thoughts further.

A word of caution: treating basic questions or sharing as mere techniques would be a disservice. Instead, genuinely tap into the unfiltered thinking in your mind and proceed from there; the initial, primitive question or experience that arises may not always be immediately apparent. To assist you in this process, here are some examples of basic, unprocessed questions: -

What precisely is the dilemma?

What truly matters to you in this situation?

What kind of decision-making process do you require?

What is the worst-case scenario?

Who would you be without this thought?

What were you noticing for yourself?

What do you get out of being the way you are now?

What are you willing to tolerate as a result?

© Ahal Besorai 2023

What story do you most often tell yourself?

What does this reveal about you?

When you ask basic questions and share your own experiences, it helps people feel more comfortable talking openly and exploring their situation further.

© Ahal Besorai 2023

Go with the flow and be positive.

"Surely only boring people went in for conversations consisting of questions and answers. The art of true conversation consisted in the play of minds."

— Ved Mehta, All for Love

This mindset is all about going with the flow and building upon what has already been said in a Forum. Think improvisational comedy (improv). In improv, if one person says, "Freeze, I have a gun" responding with, "that's not a gun, that's your finger," brings the scene to a halt. However, if you respond with, "The gun I gave you for your birthday?! I can't believe you'd use my birthday gift against me!", the scene can continue to unfold in a hilarious and engaging direction.

In a Forum setting, we may be tempted to dispute or disagree with our fellow members or express bewilderment. Some individuals are wired to find faults and be judgmental. Unfortunately, even the slightest display of judgment or negativity can shut down the conversation and discourage others from sharing their issues, thoughts, and experiences.

Positive listening is about the listener adopting a set of attitudes and using listening skills (verbal and non-verbal) that: (i) allow the listener to hear and understand exactly what is being said, and (ii) enable the person to talk freely and comfortably about problems without feeling that he/ she is being judged. Whatever is thrown at you endeavour to say - "yes and…" NOT "yes but…"

Although this might sound rather straightforward, it's so much more than - listen, accept, question and share; it's a new way of being in the world. A new mindset that is critical to effective Forum participation. It's the elegantly simple process by which we achieve and share the one thing every human innately needs for a happy, fulfilling life: connection.

Safe Conversations isn't a communication technique. It's a tool for connecting, which opens the door for clear, safe, productive communication.

In school and in our careers, we're rewarded (on top of being smart) for being good talkers. We compete for awards in public speaking and are graded on how cleverly and convincingly we convey our message. But what about listening? Where are the awards for being attentive, deeply understanding a concept, and being positive and non-judgmental?

Listening must happen for talking to matter; effective listening gives talking its true meaning.

© Ahal Besorai 2023

We may present our message eloquently, but if no one listens, it's all just words.

Listening with positivity is a demonstration of compassion and essential for connection. Think about it. Do you feel connected to someone who is being negative as you speak. Not likely. But what if they are interested, even curious about what you are telling them? Now you feel connected, as if they can relate to what you were saying and feeling. That is empathy, and there can be no genuine connection without it. Listening without judgment is the beginning of empathy.

Instead of imposing our own value systems, beliefs, or attitudes, it's crucial to embrace what the sharer says with positivity, curiosity, and a spirit of non-judgment. This does not mean blindly agreeing with everything that is shared, but maintaining an overarching attitude that whatever is raised in a Forum meeting can be addressed constructively and with respect.

From my observations, many Forum members get this wrong. I vividly recall a situation where a member wanted to discuss the difficulties they were facing with their grown son, and another participant responded with a condescending and judgment-filled "aaaannnnnd?" Such a response not only dismisses the sharer's concerns but also discourages others from opening up.

To create a supportive environment, the sharer should feel that they have a genuine partner in you. They need to believe that you are invested and committed to their well-being. Demonstrating this requires being a positive, non-judgmental listener. Make a conscious effort to shift your mindset, and even if only for the duration of the Forum session, to embody these qualities. By doing so, you create a positive emotional change that fosters trust and stability within the Forum.

Renowned psychologist Barbara Fredrickson's research emphasises the power of positive emotions. She discovered that emotions such as happiness, joy, and acceptance broaden our awareness and stimulate creative and exploratory thinking. When you respond to others with genuine positivity and without judgment, you signal to them that it's safe to share and explore what is truly going on, as well as consider new possibilities and perspectives.

Effective Forum participants not only think positively but also communicate it implicitly. Other members pick up on the safety and acceptance that such positivity creates, and they feel encouraged to contribute their thoughts and insights without fear of judgment. This inclusive and welcoming

© Ahal Besorai 2023

atmosphere enables everyone to engage in their best thinking and fosters a culture of collaboration and growth within the Forum.

© Ahal Besorai 2023

Forget Waze, ask for directions.

"I'm not sure of anything," she said. "Which is almost wonderful."

— Peter Heller, Celine

Sometime during an exploration, we find ourselves lost with no idea where to go next, what personal experience or self-curiosity to share, what question to ask or blind spot to point out. Being lost in that way is OK. It happens to all of us.

What isn't OK is to pretend to know or assume we know. When we do that, we too often start acting like the smart person in the room, the problem-solver, the answer man/woman, or the decision-maker. And when that happens, we start making assumptions and do too much steering. Another way to look at this is to realise that being the smartest person in the room probably means that you are in the wrong room…

Imagine a fellow Forum member exploring how best to parent a 14-year-old daughter with an eating disorder. As the person describes the situation, your head starts to spin and maybe you think there is no helping this kid or her parent. Your mind starts to race, "How can we move forward? Where should we go with this? I don't know what would help. Speaking of help, it's me who needs it…" As the sharer finishes setting up the description of their issue, your mind searches aimlessly for what to say next when your turn comes up.

Instead of freaking out and come out with a regurgitated statement generalising it, "normally in these situations, I ask for my wife's advice" - you can calmly, confidently and with great compassion respond with, "This sounds like a really important issue for you, what is the best way for us to get started with this?"

You are able to ask such a question because you know it's perfectly okay to ask the sharer for directions. It's OK because you believe the sharer is creative and resourceful and can make smart decisions about how the exploration should unfold.

What is happening here is a demonstration of our sincere belief in the sharer, to trust that no matter how the exploration turns out, it's OK to ask him/her for directions because our relationship is so deep.

If you are thinking ahead, you may be wondering about those times when you asked for direction and the sharer responded with "I don't know." That sort of response does not mean they aren't being creative and resourceful and capable of making smart decisions, it just means that the sharer isn't sure where to go next. No big deal. In those cases, it's probably time to

© Ahal Besorai 2023

make something up, be creative yourself, try something and see if it works.

One idea might be to do a role play where the sharer selects Forum members to take on the role of personalities involved in the issue they are facing. Another is to invite the sharer to step on to the balcony (more on that later) or share an experience you have with a similar dilemma and what it is you did and the struggle that you had to endure. All these would enable the sharer to have a fresh new perspective on the issue and possibly some way forward.

Most of the time, there will be no need to ask for directions. The sharer will make it clear where they want to go, or perhaps it's super obvious, or maybe your alert senses will be tickling. In those times, go for it and see what happens. But when you aren't sure, just know it's OK to turn off Waze and ask for directions.

© Ahal Besorai 2023

Be mindful of the potential pitfalls of empathy.

"When I get ready to talk to people, I spend two thirds of the time thinking what they need to hear and one third thinking about what I want to say."

— Abraham Lincoln

Forum is a relationship, and all good relationships need some degree of empathy – the capacity to feel and experience for yourself what another is experiencing. So, if a member shares tragic news, strong empathy would allow us to practically feel as if we were the recipient of the news. There are plenty of relationships where strong empathy is a real asset, helping build relationships and form a deep bond of trust and intimacy. Forum, for the most part, isn't one of these relationships.

This might sound surprising to some, but hang on, we need to think about empathy, vis-à-vis our Forum friends, differently than we do with others in our lives. The reason is that in a Forum context, we're here NOT to help and solve but to be helpful and facilitate – that is to say, we're here to help the sharer experience forward movement toward his/her agenda, everything else is subservient to that goal. And the problem with too much empathy is that it can distract us from that objective.

© Ahal Besorai 2023

Too much empathy puts us into the shoes of the sharer, allowing us to experience the feeling, thoughts, and perspective of that sharer. While that might sound like a positive thing to do, it's really not because then we don't provide any objective help for the sharer.

Before going any further, let me say that a Forum member who experiences a true tragedy needs a friend, a listening ear and maybe some counselling to help him/her begin to process what happened and take the first small steps toward understanding and acceptance. That isn't Forum exploration stuff in the traditional sense.

The risk of deviating from being helpful isn't caused by over empathising in the midst of a true tragedy. Rather, we deviate when a sharer has a deeply held perspective and we join him/her in that perspective. The dark side of empathy is that we can get trapped in the sharer's perspective.

Let me give an example. Suppose a sharer is having challenges with their spouse. They might be angry with the spouse because of a string of altercations and attitudes which the sharer opposes. As the sharer begins to describe the situation, too much empathy would trap us in the sharer's perspective and feelings of the situation. We would see the spouse as the "bad person" and the possibilities for forward

© Ahal Besorai 2023

movement would be severely diminished because you and the sharer are stuck in "the spouse is a bad person" perspective. In the same way the sharer cannot see a way forward from this perspective, you would not be able to be helpful by offering a fresh perspective because you would have taken his/her perspective, feelings, and account of the issue as the truth.

In this situation, the sharer has access to a truth, but not The Truth. He/she has a vantage point from which he/she can see things that are true, but he/she isn't sagacious and cannot see everything or all of what is true. Given this limited perspective, some of what he/she believes to be true may be only half-true or even false. If we join in their perspective, we fail them miserably. Our ability to remain somewhat objective is one of the greatest gifts we can give to our Forum friends because that objectivity becomes the bridge to greater insights.

Now let's be clear, being objective does not mean we see things any clearer than the sharer. It just means that we aren't locked in to their one way of experiencing the issue. Remaining objective means we can explore other perspectives and remain open and curious. Your curious stance allows you to be of great help to the sharer because from there you can

© Ahal Besorai 2023

invite them to explore options beyond what his/her locked-in perspective affords them.

In the example of the 'bad' spouse, if we're able to limit our empathy, we can maintain objectivity and invite the sharer to explore what else is going on. In essence, we can invite the sharer to step outside of his/her circumstance and comfort zone and to look at his/her feelings, thoughts, and attitudes, instead of looking at the issue through them. This shift towards a broader perspective was described by Ronald Heifitz as "getting on the balcony". This is an excellent image. Inviting the sharer to step out of their perspective by stepping onto the balcony and looking at things from a different angle. We, as listeners, aren't actually on the balcony, our objectivity merely enables us to invite the sharer to get on the balcony where he/she can see themselves and their situation more clearly.

From the balcony, the sharer might recognise his spouse's perspective in this story, the sharer's own bad behaviours and how the sharer contributed to the situation. From the balcony the sharer might reinterpret things such that his/her spouse goes from being a bad person to being a flawed human being who makes mistakes and can be selfish and is working to make his/her way through life and the relationship the best

© Ahal Besorai 2023

way he/she can (just like the sharer does). The sharer can notice and choose to believe all sorts of new things from the balcony, and he/she gets to the balcony because we employ the right Forum mindset to invite him/her to do so.

© Ahal Besorai 2023

Be Creative.

"Creativity is intelligence having fun."

— Abert Einstein

The Forum mindset involves a harmonious blend of art and science. Science and art both serve as human attempts to understand and describe the world we live in. Although they have different traditions and intended audiences, their fundamental motivations and goals are similar.

As artists, we embrace fluidity, exploration, and risk-taking to provide optimal support to our Forum friends. On the other hand, as scientists, we conduct experiments, investigate, and adhere to protocols and principles. By integrating both art and science into our Forum mindset, we unlock the creativity and potential of all Forum members. As listeners, we wear both the artist hat and the scientist hat. Each hat embodies its own form of creativity.

Consider this: our world is brimming with technologies that didn't exist even a few decades ago, such as mobile phones, solar panels, and ChatGPT. Every innovation shares a common thread: someone, somewhere had to envision these advancements. As Steve Jobs famously stated, they had to "Think different."

© Ahal Besorai 2023

The Forum mindset invites us to 'think different' and encourages our Forum friends to do the same. It entails being imaginative, experimental, vulnerable, and willing to take risks, stepping out of our comfort zones and into the realm of possibilities. Every member possesses creativity and resourcefulness, but to tap into that creative reservoir, we must also demonstrate our own creativity.

As listeners, we must avoid falling into repetitive patterns or relying solely on what has worked in previous meetings. Instead, we must fully engage in each new exploration with the specific member, at that moment, and within that unique circumstance. Creative participation demands thinking outside the box, challenging conventional boundaries, and venturing off script. It's a mindset that requires adaption and a process that improves with practice. Remember, change and being different don't happen overnight.

While Forum protocols play a critical role, especially in the formation and early stages of Forums, highly functioning Forums that embrace the correct mindset don't allow these protocols to stifle creativity.

Members of successful Forums approach their thinking in an artistic manner. By artistic, we don't mean brooding, melodramatic, tortured artists, but rather individuals who

© Ahal Besorai 2023

possess the spirit of a child with a box of crayons. Some liken it to "getting in the sandbox" – a playful and creative space where we're willing to try something new, and if it doesn't work, we simply start over and try something else.

Playful risk-taking is an integral aspect of the Forum mindset. When we, as listeners, are open to taking risks and invite the sharer to do the same, Forum magic unfolds.

Now, let's explore an example to contrast mundane, uninspired participation with a creative approach. Suppose a fellow member wishes to plan the perfect family vacation. A conventional, inside-the-box listener might ask questions like "What have you thought of so far?" or "What do you like to do?" These questions, while not terrible, still lack a spark of creativity.

A listener with a creative Forum mindset could respond by asking about the worst, most horrendous "vacation from hell" they can imagine. This question stimulates the sharer's creative juices, prompting them to approach the topic from an entirely different perspective.

Another creative Forum mindset response might be, "Let's try something different. Imagine you have returned from the vacation; all the unpacking is done, and a week later, a friend asks you about your vacation. Without mentioning any

© Ahal Besorai 2023

specific activities or locations, describe the vacation in glowing terms." By setting creative boundaries, stipulating that they cannot share what they did or where they went, it challenges the sharer to stretch their thinking beyond the conventional. Who knows what they might come up with? Perhaps they will describe the deep connections they formed with their family, how the vacation transformed their perspective, or the newfound inspiration to live life differently.

However, a word of caution is necessary. As listeners with a Forum mindset, our goal isn't to impress the sharer or our Forum friends with our own creativity. Instead, our creativity should serve as an invitation—an invitation that calls for, demands, and inspires the sharer and other Forum members to embrace their own creative potential.

Another avenue for creativity with valuable contributions for the sharer is through role-playing. In a Forum session, role-playing is a technique that simulates real-life situations or scenarios to enhance learning, problem-solving, and interpersonal skills. Participants are assigned specific roles or characters within the scenario raised by the sharer. This exercise encourages creativity and allows for a deeper understanding of various perspectives.

© Ahal Besorai 2023

A few more words on the benefits of role play in a group session:

- *Skill development*: Role play provides a safe and controlled environment for participants to practice and develop various skills, such as communication, problem-solving, negotiation, empathy, active listening, and decision-making.

- *Empathy and perspective-taking*: By assuming different roles, participants gain a better understanding of others' perspectives, needs, and challenges. This helps foster empathy and promotes a more holistic and inclusive approach to problem-solving.

- *Active engagement*: Role play encourages active participation and engagement from participants. It brings scenarios to life, making learning more immersive, dynamic, and memorable.

- *Safe exploration*: Role play allows participants to experiment with different strategies, approaches, and behaviours in a controlled setting. They can take risks, make mistakes, and learn from them without real-world consequences.

© Ahal Besorai 2023

- *Team building*: Group role play promotes collaboration, teamwork, and effective communication within the group. It fosters a sense of trust, mutual support, and shared learning experiences.

The sharer

"Do you know great minds enjoy excellence, average minds love mediocrity and small minds adore comfort zones?"

— Onyi Anyado

Without deep sharing there is no Forum.

Participating as a sharer in a Forum brings numerous benefits. It provides an opportunity to learn from diverse perspectives, receive support and empathy, gain clarity and perspective, receive constructive feedback, expand your network, develop communication and interpersonal skills, and accelerate personal growth. By actively engaging in sharing your challenges and opportunities, you tap into the collective wisdom, support, and diverse insights of fellow participants, leading to personal development, expanded connections, and valuable learning experiences.

Engaging in conversations about deeply personal issues can be a formidable task. It often involves peeling back the layers of one's emotions and experiences, revealing vulnerabilities that we may instinctively shield. The fear of judgment from others or the weight of self-criticism can loom large, acting as barriers to these discussions. Emotions, both raw and complex, often accompany personal matters, adding to the difficulty.

Despite these challenges, the act of sharing personal matters carries profound rewards. These conversations can serve as a release valve for suppressed emotions, granting a sense of relief and catharsis. Through dialogue, you can gain newfound clarity about your own thoughts and feelings, shedding light on issues that once seemed inscrutable. Sharing personal matters with your Forum colleagues can provide a valuable support system, offering comfort and reassurance. Furthermore, it can spark a transformative change or an "Aha moment", as discussions often lead to fresh insights and alternative perspectives. In the end, discussing personal matters can contribute to personal growth, healing, and a more interconnected and enriched life.

In this section of the book, we will examine the underlying motivation behind our inherent desire to grow, increase self-awareness, and tap into our hidden potential through deep sharing and receiving feedback. This drive for personal growth extends beyond Forum interactions and encompasses many aspects of our lives. We will probe into the fundamental question: Why should we bother? What compels us to invest significant effort in this pursuit?

© Ahal Besorai 2023

We shall then discuss the concept of deep sharing, what it actually means, share a few ideas about the notion of 5% sharing and give some assistance to deal with a situation where we feel we don't have a deep issue to bring to Forum.

Finally, we will conclude this part by highlighting the mindset required for effective sharing within the Forum.

Why bother?

"Hey, Ethan."

"Yeah?"

"Remember the Twinkie on the bus? The one I gave you in second grade, the day we met?"

"The one you found on the floor and gave me without telling me? Nice."

He grinned and shot the ball. "It never really fell on the floor. I made that part up."

— Kami Garcia, Beautiful Chaos

I recently came across an article recounting the story of a senior bank manager, approximately 43 years old, who received an unexpected and shocking diagnosis of Parkinson's disease. What struck me the most while reading this piece, aside from his remarkable courage and admirable outlook, was the headline that resonated deeply: – "I have Parkinson's and thank God I ran out of energy to hide it."

Indeed, maintaining a façade and refusing to acknowledge a personal struggle, such as suffering from Parkinson's disease, can demand a significant amount of energy. The act of concealing one's condition from family, friends, and even oneself can be emotionally and physically draining. It requires ongoing effort to uphold the appearance of normalcy while dealing with the underlying reality.

However, it's important to recognise that denying or avoiding a challenge does not alter its existence. In the case of the individual with Parkinson's, his refusal to acknowledge the condition did not change the fact that he was still living with the disease. The analogy of a child covering their eyes and believing they are invisible is a fitting illustration. Despite the child's belief, others can still see them.

It takes courage to confront difficult truths and seek assistance, but doing so can lead to a more authentic and empowered approach to navigating life's challenges.

Active participation in a Forum encourages us to adopt a proactive approach to life and our presence in the world. Rather than waiting until our energy is depleted, we recognise the value of preserving our vitality to bring about positive transformation. It prompts us to prioritise authentic engagement and growth, rather than expending energy on hiding or evading reality.

Our deepest calling is to embrace our authentic selves, regardless of whether it aligns with the version of ourselves that we have longed to share with the world. In doing so, we

© Ahal Besorai 2023

not only discover the joy that every human being seeks, but also uncover our path of genuine service to others.

By participating actively and authentically in a Forum, we create an environment that fosters personal growth, empathy, and understanding. We support one another in the journey of self-discovery, enabling everyone to contribute their unique perspectives and talents to the collective endeavour.

Look at the questions below, would you answer any of these in the affirmative?

- Are you feeling stuck or dissatisfied in any area of your life?
- Do you feel you fall short of reaching your full potential?
- Do you have clear goals that you want to achieve but struggle to make progress towards them?
- Are you facing recurring challenges or patterns that hinder your growth?
- Do you feel a need for greater clarity, direction, or purpose in your life?
- Would you benefit from having someone to hold you accountable and keep you on track?
- Are you open to new perspectives, feedback, and personal growth?

© Ahal Besorai 2023

- Do you feel a desire for guidance, support, and a trusted partner in your journey?

If reading these questions makes you wonder and perhaps realise that YES, there is a need to bother, to change, to improve and to grow, and this realisation brings home the reasons why it's worthwhile making an effort, feel free to proceed to the next chapter.

If you require further persuasion, let's explore an alternative approach.

"The Top Five Regrets of the Dying" is a book written by Bronnie Ware, an Australian nurse who spent several years working in palliative care. In the book, she describes the most common regrets that her patients expressed in their final days. They are:

1. "I wish I'd had the courage to live a life true to myself, not the life others expected of me."
2. "I wish I hadn't worked so hard."
3. "I wish I'd had the courage to express my feelings."
4. "I wish I had stayed in touch with my friends."
5. "I wish that I had let myself be happier."

It's a fascinating mental exercise to stop for a moment and imagine that you are on your deathbed, looking back at - your

© Ahal Besorai 2023

life values, family, friends, work, hobbies, dreams, aspirations, spirituality, children, health, emotional health, service to others, death and mortality, wisdom, financial resources, various relationships - from that perspective and simply ask yourself: -

Who is around you? Where are you? How do you feel? As you look back, what seems to matter? What do you see? How well do you believe you played the game of life, given the hand you were dealt? Do you have regrets? Are you ready to go?

How does one end life with as few regrets as possible - knowing we lived life to the full, true to ourselves, our values, and our deepest aspirations? Or perhaps more realistically, how do we end life with the right regrets...?

Personal development, afforded by effective Forum participation as a sharer, is a transformative journey, a continuous process of self-discovery, learning, and evolution. It involves embracing challenges, seeking new experiences, and expanding our perspectives. Along this path, we develop resilience, gain wisdom, and cultivate self-awareness. It's a journey that unveils our true potential, allowing us to break free from limitations and unlock new possibilities. Life growth isn't measured solely by achievements or milestones, but by the depth of our connections, the richness of our experiences,

© Ahal Besorai 2023

and the growth of our inner selves. It's an ongoing pursuit that empowers us to become the best versions of ourselves and create a meaningful impact in the world.

Theodore Roosevelt said it well: *"Nothing in the world is worth having or worth doing unless it means effort, pain, difficulty…I have never in my life envied a human being who led an easy life. I have envied a great many people who led difficult lives and led them well."*

The transformative shift emerges from within, as in –

"I tried to change the world, but I failed. I changed myself and the whole world changed."

Sharing deeply, taking off the masks, displaying vulnerability, seeking self-awareness, being open to learn, grow and change are the cornerstones for your ability to change yourself and with that to change the whole world.

© Ahal Besorai 2023

What do we mean by deep sharing?

"True connection is born out of deep conversations, where we transcend superficiality and touch the essence of each other's being."

– Unknown

<u>Introducing the ±5% sharing</u>

Deep sharing in the Forum setting refers to the +5% and -5% of data points that lie on both ends of the standard deviation graph.

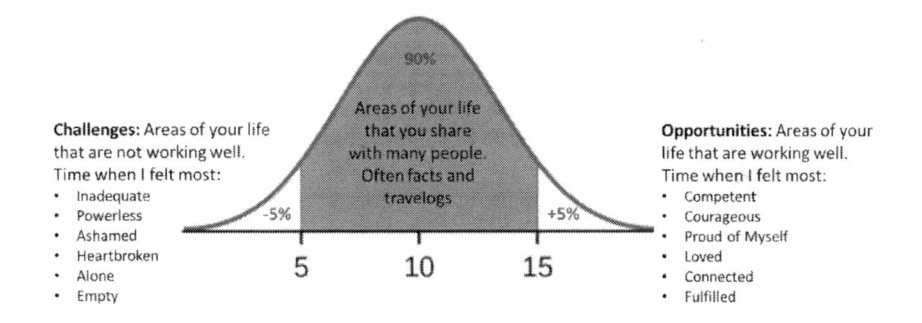

Challenges: Areas of your life that are not working well. Time when I felt most:
- Inadequate
- Powerless
- Ashamed
- Heartbroken
- Alone
- Empty

90%
Areas of your life that you share with many people. Often facts and travelogs

-5%   +5%

5   10   15

Opportunities: Areas of your life that are working well. Time when I felt most:
- Competent
- Courageous
- Proud of Myself
- Loved
- Connected
- Fulfilled

YPO Forums are designed to facilitate personal and professional growth through confidential and structured peer-to-peer learning. The primary focus is on personal growth and better self-awareness with ancillary focus on leadership development, and business-related discussions.

As individuals, we all experience a range of issues that encompass both challenges and opportunities. Moreover,

© Ahal Besorai 2023

among these issues, there exists a subset that falls within the ±5% range, which can significantly contribute to our personal growth and self-awareness if we're able to unpack and openly discuss them.

The key question then becomes: How can we facilitate the inclusion of these 5% issues in the discussions within the Forum? What kind of mindset must we adopt to encourage such a level of sharing, and what mindset is necessary for us to derive benefits from this sharing?

© Ahal Besorai 2023

A deeper look into ±5% sharing

It's interesting to recognise that the subject matter we share does not have to exclusively fall within the ±5% range. What truly matters is the substance or content of our sharing.

Let's consider the following example.

Imagine if you were to share the experience of taking a long-awaited weekend getaway with your spouse to a luxurious spa resort. You describe in detail how marvellous the place was — the delectable food, rejuvenating treatments, invigorating fresh air, etc. (they even had a pillow menu…). If the sharing concludes at this point, it could be considered a simple travelogue.

However, and this is a big however, if you then continue to share: -

Challenge 1: "and this getaway provided us with a valuable opportunity to have an open conversation about the state of our marriage. We discussed the reasons behind its difficulties and ultimately came to the realisation that, despite the potential challenges and heartache involved, it may be better for us to separate or seek external assistance to address our issues before it reaches a critical point."

Or

© Ahal Besorai 2023

Challenge 2: "and during this break, we had the possibility to engage in a meaningful conversation about our older daughter's choice of friends. It provided us with an opportunity to express our genuine concern for her well-being and explore potential solutions together. We aimed to find a resolution that not only addresses her condition but also allows us to present a united front as parents, supporting her with a shared approach that we can both rally behind."

Or

Opportunity: "and during this time away, we were granted a precious opportunity to reintroduce intimacy back into our relationship, something that kids and the demands of our busy lives prevented. It allowed us to recognise and appreciate the enduring love we still share with each other. In fact, we were even planning a second honeymoon to celebrate our (*choose a number*) year anniversary, symbolising a fresh chapter in our journey together."

The inclusion of these additional explanations regarding why the "trip to the spa" was brought up in Forum in the first place is what elevates it to a 5% sharing level, rendering it impactful and meaningful.

© Ahal Besorai 2023

5% sharing is something that might be keeping you awake at night and something that under a setting of confidentiality would be considered a unique issue to process.

5% sharing isn't something you can share over coffee or dinner with friends. The issue that you ultimately choose to work on should ideally make you feel vulnerable, slightly uncomfortable and feeling that you are taking a risk by sharing.

A litmus test one may apply would be to consider asking yourself the following questions:

1. Is the issue I'm bringing to the Forum important, urgent, emotional, painful, or impactful?

2. Does it drain a lot of my energy? and

3. Does it hold significant potential for personal growth and opportunity once I unravel it?

Brené Brown summed it up beautifully when asserting that vulnerability is the birthplace of connection and the path to the feeling of worthiness. Hence, if it doesn't feel vulnerable, the sharing is probably not constructive.

I'm still grappling with the opportunity or challenge to present to my Forum.

In some cases, especially when Forum meetings are frequent, you may find yourself without a new issue that fits the criteria

© Ahal Besorai 2023

mentioned earlier. This is perfectly fine. It's important to avoid artificially creating topics solely to meet the expectation of contributing substantially or to demonstrate a particular level of depth and vulnerability. Instead, think creatively and don't feel constrained by structures and rules.

For example, consider expanding your focus beyond the usual 60-day time frame. The Forum serves as an excellent platform for addressing long-standing issues that we may have carried with us but never had the opportunity to properly acknowledge, discuss, and resolve.

Take, for instance, the personal changes you might wish to make. This could involve habits like impatience, resentment, difficulty expressing emotions, or a feeling that you need to invest more effort in nurturing and cultivating relationships. Alternatively, you might choose to confront past traumas which have been impeding your potential to experience life to the fullest.

You can also engage in a simple exercise of envisioning your goals and aspirations for the next 3-5 (or 15) years and discuss the necessary steps, adjustments, or changes required to reach them. There are always areas in our lives where we can strive for self-improvement, and the Forum provides a unique space for exploring and unpacking these issues. Each of these

© Ahal Besorai 2023

matters is deserving of Forum discussion, as both you and your Forum stand to gain valuable insights and personal growth from such exploration.

When introducing such topics, you can examine how these issues have influenced or hindered your various life endeavours. You can reflect on whether these traits serve you and why, or if not, explore actions that can be taken to eliminate or at least manage these habits. Other Forum members can contribute by sharing their own experiences with similar traits or other challenges they feel trapped by. Additionally, you could consider what kind of support and accountability measures the Forum, or a chosen member of the Forum, can provide to assist you in implementing the proposed actions.

© Ahal Besorai 2023

The Sharer Mindset

"Strength is not only measured by how much you can handle alone but also by how much you can share with others."

– Unknown

We all have 'issues' because we all have a story. And no matter how much work you have done on yourself, we all snap back sometimes. So be easy on yourself. Growth is a dance. Not a light switch. In a sense, it's a beautiful thing that we do have issues because this crack in everything is how the light gets in.

As we have emphasised before, a Forum relies on deep sharing within the ±5%. To further reiterate, it's not necessary for each participant to have issues to discuss in every meeting. However, it's expected that each individual maintains at least one issue in the Parking Lot, which can then be scheduled for future Forum meetings by the moderator.

On numerous occasions, I have come across Forum members who have summoned the courage and raised an issue within the ±5%. but, out of a sense of modesty or deference, expressed statements like, "the issue of another Forum member seems more important than mine, so they should go

© Ahal Besorai 2023

first"; giving priority to a Forum colleague's issue to be explored instead of theirs.

Please, don't do that! Advocate fiercely for your issue to be thoroughly explored and examined.

The Forum serves as a transformative space where personal growth is nurtured in a profound and meaningful manner. As a potential sharer, it's essential to seize that opportunity and make the most of it. Fight for the chance to unpack your issue and benefit from the collective experiences and support of your Forum companions. Embrace the potential for growth and transformation that the Forum offers.

When you are called upon to explore your topic from the parking lot, or perhaps when you have just raised an important and urgent matter during the updates that you wish to explore, it's crucial to ensure that you are prepared, willing, and motivated to embrace the opportunity for learning, growth, and improvement. Understand that the process of exploration can yield valuable insights, provide support, and foster accountability to facilitate your journey.

This required mindset serves as the foremost prerequisite for a successful exploration. The drive and energy you exhibit while working towards your goal stem from the motivation you cultivate within yourself. Remember, it's entirely

© Ahal Besorai 2023

dependent on you to nurture and maintain that motivation throughout the process.

Your willingness and motivation exemplify a proactive mindset, commitment to personal growth, and willingness to actively engage in the exploration process to achieve positive change and desired outcomes.

While one approach to unpacking an issue is to follow the YPO 4-step exploration module, it's important to note that alternative exploration methods are also available. The choice of exploration method ultimately rests with the explorer and the Forum, as they collaborate to determine the approach that best suits their needs.

Before proceeding to discuss the sharer's requisite mindset, allow me to present a useful distinction between two types of exploration - exploration for performance and exploration for development.

Exploration for performance revolves around addressing and resolving a specific problem or challenge. It entails taking action to address, enhance, or manage the immediate issue at hand. This type of exploration is focused on everyday tasks and issues, playing a vital role in problem-solving. Issues like – writing a will, building effective leadership skills, strengthening resilience, managing stress, improving conflict

© Ahal Besorai 2023

resolution and negotiation skills are some such performance issues.

On the other hand, **exploration for development** shifts the emphasis from the immediate issue to the individual managing the issue. It transcends the mere resolution of the problem and directs attention toward the personal growth and development of the individual. These conversations hold significant transformative power. When you reflect on moments where an exploration truly made a difference, it's likely that it was an exploration for development rather than a solely performance oriented one. In those instances, the focus was on encouraging the sharer to learn, improve, and grow, rather than solely on resolving the immediate matter.

By emphasising development, the conversation invites individuals to expand their understanding, challenge their assumptions, and embrace new perspectives. It creates space for self-reflection, personal growth, and ongoing learning. While exploration for performance is important for handling immediate challenges, exploration for development offers a more profound and transformative approach. It holds the power to facilitate lasting change and growth, surpassing mere surface-level issue resolution and instead fostering continuous improvement and personal development.

© Ahal Besorai 2023

In Forum, the majority of explorations needs to be explorations for development.

Regardless of the exploration method or whether the issue relates to performance or development, it's imperative for the sharer to address the following questions when presenting the issue to the Forum: -

- What is the specific nature of your issue? What is the exact dilemma?
- Why is this topic important to you?
- What emotions does it evoke within you?
- What is getting in the way of you resolving it?

When it comes to the mindset of the person sharing an issue in a Forum, it's vital to embrace the following: -

1. **Openness and receptivity:** Be open to receiving support, feedback, and insights from Forum members. Approach the sharing process with a willingness to hear different perspectives and consider alternative viewpoints. Openness allows you to receive valuable input that can contribute to your personal growth and problem-solving.

2. **Vulnerability and honesty:** Embrace vulnerability by being authentic and transparent about your

issue. Share your experiences, emotions, and challenges openly, allowing others to understand your situation fully. Honesty fosters trust and encourages others to engage with empathy and support.

3. **Humility and a learning orientation:** Adopt a humble mindset that acknowledges that you don't have all the answers. Be willing to learn from the collective wisdom and experiences of others in the Forum. Recognise that sharing an issue is an opportunity for growth and improvement, and approach it with a genuine desire to learn and evolve.

4. **Willingness to receive feedback:** In Forum, the rule is that the feedback isn't given but is requested. As such, feedback is an option which you as sharer can activate. Be receptive to feedback and different perspectives. Understand that feedback is an opportunity for growth and self-reflection. Listen actively to the insights and suggestions provided by Forum members, even if they challenge your existing beliefs or assumptions.

5. **Focus on solutions and growth:** Maintain a positive and solution-oriented mindset. While sharing your

issue, express a desire to find resolutions, overcome challenges, and grow from the experience. Frame your sharing in a way that invites constructive suggestions and strategies from others.

6. **Trust in your Forum colleagues:** Trust in the support and confidentiality of your Forum. Feel assured that your issue will be treated with respect and that the members are there to offer guidance and assistance. Trusting the Forum environment allows you to fully engage and benefit from the collective wisdom of the group.

By embracing this mindset, the person sharing an issue can create a supportive space for themselves and invite meaningful contributions from others, enhancing the potential for personal growth and problem-solving within the Forum.

© Ahal Besorai 2023

About the Author

Ahal Besorai

YPO and the Forum have played a pivotal and meaningful role in my personal journey and development. My 20+ years of Forum experiences have shown me that vulnerability and profound sharing aren't just about taking risks; they are, in fact, a privilege. True living begins at the edge of our comfort zones, and vulnerability serves as a potent tool to push us to that precipice.

When working with Forums, my objective extends beyond ensuring that every YPO Forum member experiences a touch of that "Forum Magic" within their current Forum. I strive to generate forward momentum within each Forum, ensuring that subsequent, non-facilitated Forum meetings are equally deep and meaningful. I aspire to empower every Forum to operate at a level that aligns with its members' comfort, equipped with the requisite mindset, tools, protocols, and norms to extract genuine value from each gathering.

My extensive background spans diverse realms, including the kibbutz, military, academia, and the business world. This journey has not only equipped me with a solid foundation of knowledge and experience but has also instilled in me a deep sense of humanity and compassion, serving as a counterbalance to my "hard" skills. This balance enables me to effectively guide Forums and their members towards their desired destinations.

Presently, I call the Philippines my home, residing just outside Manila. I cherish the people, the vibrant culture, the delectable cuisine, and all the unique aspects of this beautiful country. My main Forum affiliation lies with the YPO Gold Philippines chapter, and I'm also a member of two additional Forums. This privilege fuels my desire to assist other Forums achieve Forum Magic, not only in the Philippines but also across Asia and the rest of the world.

© Ahal Besorai 2023

Disclaimer

I would like to begin by expressing my sincere apologies if, in the process of creating this book, I inadvertently included any material that isn't my own. As an author, I understand the importance of respecting intellectual property rights and the value of originality.

While every effort has been made to ensure the authenticity and originality of the content presented in this book, there is always a possibility of unintentional oversight or oversight in the referencing process. I assure you that it was never my intention to appropriate or misattribute any ideas, concepts, or text without proper acknowledgment.

I would like to emphasise that any resemblance to existing works, whether intentional or unintentional, is purely coincidental. I have strived to produce a unique and original piece of literature, drawing upon my own experiences, research, and creativity. However, I acknowledge that inspiration can come from various sources, and I may have unconsciously incorporated elements that are similar to pre-existing works.

© Ahal Besorai 2023

If it comes to your attention that any part of this book includes content that isn't properly attributed or violates any copyright or intellectual property laws, I urge you to bring it to my attention so that appropriate measures can be taken to rectify the situation. Your feedback and assistance are highly valued in upholding the integrity of this work and ensuring the respect of the creative community.

Please understand that the opinions, views, and ideas expressed in this book are solely those of the author and should not be misconstrued as endorsements or factual statements unless explicitly stated otherwise. It's important to exercise critical thinking and personal judgment when engaging with any written work.

I would like to extend my gratitude to all the individuals, scholars, and creators who have contributed to the vast landscape of knowledge and creativity. Their work has undoubtedly influenced the broader understanding of the topics covered in this book.

Thank you for your understanding, and I hope that you find this book insightful, enjoyable, and worthy of your time.

© Ahal Besorai 2023

Acknowledgements

First and foremost, I would like to express my deepest gratitude to YPO (Young Presidents' Organisation) for providing a platform that has allowed me to engage in Forums and embark on a remarkable journey of personal growth. The opportunities and experiences facilitated by YPO have been instrumental in shaping my understanding of effective Forum participation.

To my incredible Forum buddies within YPO, I'm immensely grateful for your unwavering support, camaraderie, and the transformative impact you have had on my life. Your wisdom, vulnerability, and willingness to challenge and uplift one another have been truly extraordinary. It's through our shared experiences and profound connections that I have grown both personally and professionally. Thank you for embracing me into the fold and infecting me with the remarkable spirit of the Forum.

I would also like to extend a special appreciation to the individuals who have played an integral role in shaping my understanding of Forum dynamics and mindset. Your contributions have been invaluable, and I'm deeply grateful for your insights and guidance.

© Ahal Besorai 2023

To Alex von Baer, Sandeep Walia, Mukesh Mehta, Karen Morais, Wai Ming and to my son, Emanuel Besorai, your wisdom, expertise, and unwavering dedication to fostering meaningful Forum experiences have left an indelible mark on my journey. Thank you for sharing your knowledge, challenging my perspectives, and for being shining examples of what effective Forum participation entails.

Lastly, but certainly not least, I want to extend my gratitude to the readers of this short eBook. Your curiosity, engagement, and willingness to explore effective Forum participation are truly commendable. It's my sincere hope that the insights shared within these pages will empower you to approach Forums with the right mindset and embrace the transformative power they offer.

With heartfelt gratitude and a deep appreciation for the Forum community,

Ahal Besorai

© Ahal Besorai 2023

Exercise Bank

The exercises below follow the chapters of the book.

Be patient.

Exercise: Cultivating Patience and Empathy for Colleagues' Vulnerability

Duration: Approximately 30-45 minutes

Materials needed: Writing materials for participants.

Instructions:

1. *Introduction (5 minutes)*
   - Gather all participants and explain the purpose of the exercise.
   - Emphasize the importance of patience and empathy in fostering a supportive and inclusive Forum environment.
   - Highlight the challenges some colleagues may face in opening up and being vulnerable. (Fear of judgment, Past negative experiences, Cultural

or societal norms, Self-preservation instincts, Lack of trust, Perceived professional image)

2. *Reflection (10 minutes)*

    o Ask each participant to take a few minutes to reflect on a time when they felt vulnerable or hesitant to open up in a professional setting.

    o Encourage participants to write down their thoughts and feelings about the experience.

    o Remind them that vulnerability can be challenging and varies from person to person.

3. *Sharing Personal Experiences (15 minutes)*

    o Divide participants into pairs or small groups.

    o Instruct each participant to share their reflection on the past vulnerability experience with their partner or group members.

    o Encourage active listening and create a safe space for participants to express their thoughts and emotions without judgment.

    o Remind participants to be patient and attentive to their partners' stories.

© Ahal Besorai 2023

4. *Perspective-Taking (10 minutes)*
    - After sharing their experiences, instruct participants to imagine themselves in their colleagues' shoes, specifically those who find it difficult to open up and be vulnerable.
    - Encourage participants to think about the potential reasons or barriers that may prevent their colleagues from being more forthcoming.
    - Ask participants to write down their thoughts on how they would feel and what challenges they might face if they were in their colleagues' position.

5. *Group Discussion (10 minutes)*
    - Bring the participants back together as a whole group.
    - Facilitate a discussion by asking volunteers to share their insights and perspectives gained from the exercise.
    - Encourage participants to discuss strategies for cultivating patience and empathy towards colleagues who struggle with vulnerability.

- Highlight the importance of creating a supportive environment that encourages open communication and respect for different comfort levels.

6. *Action Planning (5 minutes)*
    - Conclude the exercise by asking participants to individually write down one action they can take to demonstrate patience and empathy towards their colleagues who find it difficult to open up.
    - Encourage participants to set a realistic timeline for implementing their action plan.

Closing:

- Thank all participants for their active engagement and willingness to explore the topic of patience and empathy in the workplace.
- Reinforce the importance of creating a supportive and inclusive work culture where vulnerability is respected and valued.
- Encourage participants to implement their action plans and reflect on their progress in future interactions with their colleagues.

© Ahal Besorai 2023

Note: The suggested timeframe is approximate and can be adjusted based on the depth of discussion desired. Ensure that all participants have the opportunity to share their reflections and insights during the exercise.

Come wearing a white belt.

Exercise: Embracing the White Belt Mindset in Forum Meetings

Duration: Approximately 20-30 minutes

Materials needed: Writing materials for participants.

Instructions:

1. **Introduction (5 minutes)**
    - Explain the purpose of the exercise.
    - Introduce the concept of the "white belt" mindset, which represents approaching meetings with a beginner's mindset, open to learning and new ideas.
    - Emphasize the importance of humility, active listening, and the willingness to ask questions.

2. **Reflection on Assumptions (5 minutes)**
    - Ask participants to take a few minutes to reflect on their typical mindset and behaviours in meetings.

© Ahal Besorai 2023

- o Encourage them to consider any assumptions, preconceived notions, or biases they may bring into meetings that could hinder collaboration and learning.
- o Instruct participants to write down their reflections.

3. **White Belt Mindset Affirmations (10 minutes)**
    - o Provide participants with a list of affirmations related to the white belt mindset. Some examples include:
        - "I'm open to new perspectives and ideas."
        - "I embrace the opportunity to learn from others."
        - "I actively listen to understand, not just to respond."
        - "I ask questions to deepen my understanding and encourage dialogue."
    - o Ask participants to choose one or two affirmations that resonate with them and write them down.

- Encourage participants to reflect on these affirmations and how they can embody them in their approach to Forum meetings.

4. *Small Group Discussion (10 minutes)*
    - Divide the group into pairs or have a group discussion if number of participants is small.
    - Instruct each participant to discuss their chosen affirmations and share personal experiences or challenges they anticipate in practicing the white belt mindset.
    - Encourage participants to offer suggestions and support to one another, sharing strategies for overcoming potential barriers to adopting a white belt mindset.

5. *Whole Group Sharing (5 minutes)*
    - Bring the participants back together as a whole group.
    - Ask volunteers to share their affirmations and insights gained from the pair discussions.
    - Facilitate a brief discussion, allowing participants to share their thoughts on the

© Ahal Besorai 2023

benefits of adopting a white belt mindset in meetings and how it can enhance collaboration and learning.

Closing:

- Thank all participants for their active engagement in the exercise and their willingness to embrace the white belt mindset.

- Encourage participants to regularly remind themselves of their chosen affirmations before attending meetings.

- Emphasize the value of continuous learning, curiosity, and humility in fostering a productive and inclusive meeting culture.

Note: The exercise duration can be adjusted based on the depth of discussion desired. Encourage participants to practice the white belt mindset not only in meetings but also in their daily interactions, fostering a growth-oriented and collaborative mindset in their work.

© Ahal Besorai 2023

Curiosity in, judgement out

Exercise: Cultivating Curiosity

One Thing for You to Think About:

Consider the profound impact of curiosity on various aspects of your life:

- Curiosity Cures: It alleviates anxiety, ignorance, selfishness, and extremism.
- Curiosity Creates: It fosters empathy, compassion, knowledge, and personal growth.
- Curiosity Prevents: It guards against arrogance, judgment, and stagnation.

Now, let's practice curiosity.

One Thing for You to Ask Yourself:

Reflect on where in your life you could benefit from being more curious. This curiosity could be directed toward:

- The People Around You: Seek to understand their perspectives and experiences.
- The World or Society You Live In: Explore the complexities and nuances of your environment.

- The Person You Spend the Most Time With: Delve deeper into their thoughts, feelings, and dreams.

Imagine the possibilities if you were more curious in that area. How might it transform your interactions and understanding?

One Thing for You to Try This Week:

This week, make a conscious effort to practice curiosity. Here's how:

- **Ask Interesting Questions**: Challenge yourself to ask thought-provoking questions of others, yourself, and about life and the world.
- **Seek Answers**: After asking questions, actively seek answers. Dive into research, conversations, or personal exploration to find responses.
- **Question the Answers**: Don't stop at the initial answers you uncover. Ask whether those answers could be incomplete or incorrect. Challenge assumptions.
- **Observe Organic Changes**: Pay attention to the changes that naturally unfold around you as you embrace curiosity. Notice how it affects your relationships, knowledge, and personal growth.

While practicing curiosity, notice the changes that organically emerge around you.

© Ahal Besorai 2023

Exercise: Curiosity Walk (good for a retreat)

Duration: Approximately 30-45 minutes

Materials needed: None.

Instructions:

1. *Introduction (5 minutes)*
     - Explain the purpose of the exercise.
     - Emphasize the importance of cultivating curiosity and open-mindedness in daily life generally and Forum particularly.
     - Highlight how this exercise aims to encourage participants to observe and explore their surroundings with a curious mindset.

2. *Setting the Intention (5 minutes)*
     - Ask participants to take a moment to set their intention for the exercise.
     - Encourage them to focus on being present, observing their environment, and seeking out interesting details or experiences.
     - Instruct participants to mentally commit to approaching the exercise with a curious mindset.

© Ahal Besorai 2023

3. **Curiosity Walk (20-30 minutes)**
    - Instruct participants to go on a walk individually or in pairs, depending on the size of the group.
    - Encourage participants to choose a route that they find interesting or unfamiliar.
    - Instruct them to pay attention to their surroundings, engage their senses, and actively seek out things that pique their curiosity.
    - Encourage participants to ask questions, explore their environment, and make note of any observations or insights.

4. **Group Sharing and Reflection (10 minutes)**
    - Gather all participants at the end of the walk.
    - Invite each participant to share one or two interesting things they noticed or discovered during their walk.
    - Encourage participants to reflect on how the exercise affected their mindset, level of curiosity, and awareness of their surroundings.

© Ahal Besorai 2023

- Facilitate a brief discussion to explore common themes or observations shared by the participants.

Closing:

- Thank all participants for their active engagement in the exercise and their willingness to cultivate curiosity.
- Encourage participants to carry the curiosity they experienced during the exercise into their daily lives.
- Remind them that curiosity can be nurtured through observation, questioning, and engaging with the world around them.

Note: Adjust the duration of the walk based on the available time and the surroundings. Encourage participants to approach the exercise with an open mind and a genuine desire to explore and discover new things.

Exercise: Cultivating Curiosity

Duration: Approximately 20-30 minutes

Materials needed: Writing materials for participants.

Instructions:

1. *Introduction (5 minutes)*

- Explain the purpose of the exercise.
- Emphasize the importance of curiosity in personal and professional growth, fostering creativity, and building meaningful relationships.
- Highlight the benefits of being open-minded, asking questions, and seeking new knowledge and perspectives.

2. **Reflection on Personal Curiosity (5 minutes)**
    - Ask participants to take a few minutes to reflect on their current level of curiosity and their mindset towards learning and exploring new ideas.
    - Encourage them to consider areas where they feel curious and areas where they may benefit from cultivating more curiosity.
    - Instruct participants to write down their reflections.

3. **Curiosity Journal (10 minutes)**
    - Provide participants with a blank journal or notebook pages.

- Explain that they will use this journal to record their curious thoughts, questions, and observations.

- Encourage participants to carry the journal with them throughout the day or week, capturing moments of curiosity and jotting down questions that arise.

- Remind participants to write freely and without judgment, allowing their curiosity to guide their exploration.

4. *Pair Sharing (10 minutes)*

    - Pair up participants randomly.

    - Instruct each pair to take turns sharing one curious thought, question, or observation from their journal with each other.

    - Encourage active listening and genuine curiosity in response to their partner's sharing.

    - Allow sufficient time for each participant to share and receive feedback.

5. *Personal Action Plan (5 minutes)*

© Ahal Besorai 2023

- Conclude the exercise by asking participants to individually reflect on how they can incorporate curiosity into their daily lives.

- Instruct them to write down one or two specific actions they will take to cultivate curiosity, such as reading a new genre of books, attending a seminar on a topic of interest, or engaging in conversations with people from diverse backgrounds.

- Encourage participants to set a realistic timeline for implementing their action plan.

Closing:

- Thank all participants for their active participation in the exercise and their commitment to developing curiosity.

- Emphasize that curiosity is a lifelong journey and encourage participants to continue nurturing their curiosity in various aspects of their lives.

- Remind participants to revisit their curiosity journal regularly and celebrate their growth and discoveries along the way.

© Ahal Besorai 2023

Note: The exercise duration can be adjusted based on the depth of discussion desired. Encourage participants to embrace curiosity beyond the exercise and make it a daily practice in their personal and professional lives.

To advise or not to advise

Exercise: "Advice-Free Zone"

Duration: Approximately 20-30 minutes

Materials needed: Paper or index cards, writing materials.

Instructions:

1. *Introduction (5 minutes)*

    - Explain the purpose of the exercise.
    - Highlight the tendency to give advice when someone shares a problem or challenge.
    - Emphasize the importance of creating a space where advice is temporarily suspended, allowing for deeper exploration and understanding.

2. *Scenario Creation (5 minutes)*

    - Distribute paper or index cards to each participant.
    - Instruct participants to individually write down a personal challenge or problem they are currently facing.

© Ahal Besorai 2023

- Encourage them to keep their challenges concise and focused.

3. **Pair Sharing (10-15 minutes)**

    - Pair up participants randomly.
    - Instruct each pair to take turns sharing their challenge without the listener offering any advice or solutions.
    - Encourage the listener to practice active listening, asking open-ended questions for clarification, and providing non-verbal cues to show understanding and support.
    - Remind participants that the goal is to fully listen and empathize rather than providing advice.

4. **Reflection and Discussion (5 minutes)**

    - Bring the participants back together as a group.
    - Facilitate a brief discussion by asking the following questions:
        - How did it feel to share your challenge without receiving immediate advice or solutions?

- How did it feel to listen without the need to give advice?

- What did you notice about the conversation when advice was not offered?

- Did you gain any insights or deeper understanding through the exercise?

Closing:

- Thank all participants for their active engagement in the exercise and their willingness to explore a space without advice-giving.

- Emphasize the importance of active listening and empathy in supporting others.

- Encourage participants to carry the experience from the exercise into their daily interactions, being mindful of the impulse to offer advice, and to practice deep listening.

Note: The duration of each phase can be adjusted based on the number of participants and the depth of discussion desired. Remind participants that the purpose of the exercise is to create a supportive space for reflection and understanding,

© Ahal Besorai 2023

allowing individuals to share their challenges without the pressure of receiving immediate advice.

© Ahal Besorai 2023

Be positive.

Exercise: "Yes, And... Stay Positive"

Duration: Approximately 20-30 minutes

Materials needed: None.

Instructions:

1. *Introduction (5 minutes)*
    - Explain the purpose of the exercise.
    - Emphasize the importance of going with the flow, embracing spontaneity, and maintaining a positive mindset.
    - Explain that the exercise is inspired by improv techniques and aims to help participants practice accepting and building upon each other's ideas while staying positive.

2. *Circle Formation (5 minutes)*
    - Arrange the participants in a circle, ensuring that everyone can see and hear each other.
    - Encourage participants to create an open and supportive space where everyone feels comfortable contributing.

3. **Prompt Setting (5 minutes)**
   - Start by providing a simple prompt or scenario related to a specific theme or topic.
   - For example, "You are planning a surprise party for a friend."
   - Explain that each participant will take turns adding a positive statement or idea related to the prompt, building upon the contributions of others.

4. **"Yes, And... Stay Positive" (10-15 minutes)**
   - Begin the exercise by having the first participant share a positive statement related to the prompt.
   - The next participant must then respond with a positive "Yes, and..." statement, building upon the previous contribution.
   - Encourage participants to focus on adding value, staying positive, and accepting and building upon the ideas of others.
   - Remind participants that the goal is to create a positive and collaborative narrative together.

5. **Reflection and Discussion (5 minutes)**

© Ahal Besorai 2023

- Bring the exercise to a close and gather all participants for a brief discussion.
- Facilitate a reflection by asking the following questions:
  - How did it feel to go with the flow and maintain a positive mindset during the exercise?
  - What challenges did you encounter in accepting and building upon each other's ideas while staying positive?
  - How can you apply the principles of "Yes, and... stay positive" in your daily interactions to foster collaboration and a positive outlook?

Closing:

- Thank all participants for their active engagement in the exercise and their commitment to going with the flow and staying positive.
- Highlight the importance of embracing spontaneity, building upon each other's ideas, and maintaining a positive mindset.

© Ahal Besorai 2023

- Encourage participants to practice the "Yes, and... stay positive" approach in their personal and professional lives, fostering collaboration, creativity, and a positive atmosphere.

Note: Adjust the duration of each phase based on the number of participants and the depth of discussion desired. Remind participants to actively listen, respond positively, and build upon the ideas shared by others. Emphasize the supportive and non-judgmental nature of the exercise, promoting a safe and positive environment. Encourage participants to let go of self-consciousness and embrace the collective creativity of the group while maintaining a positive outlook.

Alternative Prompts

1. Prompt: "You are planning a quirky theme party."
   - Participants can add funny and offbeat ideas for the theme, costumes, decorations, and activities that would make the party memorable and hilarious.

2. Prompt: "You are organizing a wacky talent show."
   - Participants can contribute funny and unusual talents or acts that performers can showcase

© Ahal Besorai 2023

during the talent show, encouraging laughter and amusement.

3. Prompt: "You are creating a comedic sketch."

    o Participants can share funny scenarios, dialogues, and punchlines to create an entertaining and humorous sketch that will have everyone laughing.

4. Prompt: "You are designing a silly invention."

    o Participants can come up with absurd and comical ideas for inventions that serve bizarre or hilarious purposes, adding humor to the exercise.

5. Prompt: "You are hosting a fictional awards ceremony for unusual achievements."

    o Participants can suggest funny and outlandish categories for awards, along with humorous acceptance speeches and outrageous moments at the ceremony.

© Ahal Besorai 2023

It's Netflix time.

Exercise: The Hero's Journey

Duration: Approximately 30-45 minutes

Materials needed: Flipchart paper or whiteboard, markers, sticky notes.

Instructions:

1. **Introduction (5 minutes)**
   - Explain the purpose of the exercise.
   - Emphasize the importance of creating a supportive environment where the presenter of a personal issue can feel empowered and remain the hero of the discussion.
   - Explain that the exercise aims to explore different perspectives, insights, and support for the presenter while maintaining a focus on their growth and development.

2. **Storytelling (15 minutes)**
   - Designate one participant as the "Presenter" or the "Hero" for the exercise.

- Instruct the Presenter to share a personal issue or challenge they are facing. Encourage them to provide context, details, and emotions associated with their story.
- As the Presenter shares their story, write down key points on flipchart paper or a whiteboard to help visualize the narrative.

3. *Appreciative Inquiry (10-15 minutes)*

    - Divide the remaining participants into small groups of 3-4 people.
    - Assign each group a specific aspect or theme related to the Presenter's story (e.g., strengths, opportunities, resources, resilience).
    - Instruct each group to discuss and brainstorm positive aspects related to their assigned theme.
    - Encourage participants to focus on the strengths, qualities, and progress made by the Presenter.

4. *Hero's Support (10 minutes)*

    - After the small group discussions, bring the participants back together as a whole group.

© Ahal Besorai 2023

- Ask each small group to share the positive aspects they identified based on their assigned theme.

- Encourage participants to offer supportive comments, encouragement, and insights to the Presenter, highlighting their strengths and acknowledging their journey.

5. Reflection and Action (5-10 minutes)

    - Facilitate a brief discussion by asking the Presenter to reflect on the insights and support received.

    - Ask the Presenter to identify one or two action steps they can take based on the positive aspects and support shared during the exercise.

    - Encourage the Presenter to share their commitment and invite any additional feedback or suggestions from the group.

Closing:

- Thank all participants for their active engagement in the exercise and their support of the Presenter's journey.

© Ahal Besorai 2023

- Highlight the power of positive perspectives and collective support in empowering the Presenter to remain the hero of their own story.

- Encourage participants to carry the spirit of support and empowerment into their daily interactions, celebrating the strengths and growth of others.

Note: Adjust the duration of each phase based on the number of participants and the depth of discussion desired. Remind participants to provide constructive and uplifting feedback, focusing on the Presenter's growth and development. Emphasize the importance of maintaining a supportive and non-judgmental environment throughout the exercise.

© Ahal Besorai 2023

Go raw, process less.

Exercise: Unfiltered Reflection

Duration: Approximately 20-30 minutes

Materials needed: Paper or index cards, writing materials.

Instructions:

1. ***Introduction (5 minutes)***

    - Explain the purpose of the exercise.
    - Emphasize the importance of simplicity and authenticity in sharing observations, experiences, thoughts, and reflections.
    - Explain that the exercise aims to encourage participants to express themselves without filters or overthinking.

2. ***Observation Walk (5 minutes)***

    - Instruct participants to individually take a short walk around the room or outside, focusing on their surroundings.
    - Encourage them to observe the environment, paying attention to details, sights, sounds, and sensations.

3. **Unfiltered Reflection (10-15 minutes)**
    - Distribute paper or index cards to each participant.
    - Instruct participants to write down their unfiltered observations, experiences, thoughts, and reflections from the walk.
    - Encourage them to keep their responses simple, concise, and unedited. Remind them not to overthink or filter their thoughts.

4. **Sharing Circle (5-10 minutes)**
    - Form a circle with all participants.
    - Invite each participant to share one observation, experience, thought, or reflection from their card without elaborating or adding additional commentary.
    - Encourage active listening without interruptions or judgment as each participant shares their unfiltered reflections.

5. **Reflection and Discussion (5 minutes)**
    - Facilitate a brief discussion by asking the following questions:

© Ahal Besorai 2023

- How did it feel to express your thoughts and reflections without filtering or overthinking?
- What did you notice about the simplicity and authenticity of the shared reflections?
- Did you gain any new insights or perspectives through this exercise?

Closing:

- Thank all participants for their active participation in the exercise and their willingness to share unfiltered reflections.
- Emphasize the value of simplicity and authenticity in communication and self-expression.
- Encourage participants to incorporate this practice of unfiltered reflection into their daily lives, fostering greater authenticity and openness in their interactions.

Note: The duration of each phase can be adjusted based on the number of participants and the depth of discussion desired. Remind participants that the purpose of the exercise is to cultivate a sense of simplicity and authenticity in sharing their observations, experiences, thoughts, and reflections.

© Ahal Besorai 2023

Encourage them to let go of self-judgment and perfectionism, allowing their unfiltered reflections to emerge naturally.

A guide to asking good questions.

Here's more specific guidance on how to form good questions to assist participants:

1. Start with open-ended questions: Begin your coaching questions with "What," "How," "Tell me about," or "Describe." These types of questions encourage the sharer to provide detailed responses and explore their thoughts and feelings.

2. Focus on the sharer's perspective: Frame your questions to elicit the sharer's own insights and perspectives. Avoid leading or biased questions that push them towards a particular answer. Allow them to think critically and explore their own understanding of the situation.

3. Ask for specific examples: Request concrete examples or instances to help the sharer illustrate their experiences or challenges. This can provide clarity and enable deeper exploration of the situation.

4. Explore assumptions and beliefs: Encourage the sharer to examine their underlying assumptions, beliefs, and

© Ahal Besorai 2023

values related to the topic at hand. Ask questions that challenge their assumptions and prompt them to consider alternative perspectives.

5. Encourage reflection and self-awareness: Pose questions that prompt the sharer to reflect on their thoughts, emotions, and behaviours. Help them gain self-awareness by asking questions like, "What impact do you think your behavior has on others?" or "How does this situation align with your values?"

6. Clarify goals and aspirations: Help the sharer articulate their desired outcomes and goals. Ask questions that explore what they want to achieve, why it's important to them, and how they envision success.

7. Probe deeper with follow-up questions: Listen actively to the sharer's responses and use follow-up questions to delve deeper into their thinking and explore different angles. For example, you can ask, "Can you tell me more about that?" or "What other options have you considered?"

8. Balance challenge and support: Effective coaching questions strike a balance between challenging the sharer to think critically and supporting them in their exploration. Foster an environment of trust and respect

© Ahal Besorai 2023

and adapt your questioning style to meet the sharer's needs.

Remember, good coaching questions are meant to facilitate the sharer's thinking and promote self-discovery. They should encourage exploration, reflection, and actionable insights. By practicing and refining your questioning skills, you can become more adept at guiding others through the coaching process.

© Ahal Besorai 2023

Exercise: A Raw Mind

Duration: Approximately 20-30 minutes

Materials needed: None.

Instructions:

1. **Introduction (5 minutes)**

    - Explain the purpose of the exercise.

    - Emphasize the importance of approaching personal issues with a beginner's mind, free from assumptions and preconceived notions.

    - Explain that the exercise aims to train participants to ask basic, unprocessed questions to better understand and support their colleagues.

2. **Pairing Up (5 minutes)**

    - Pair up participants randomly.

    - Instruct each pair to decide who will take the role of the "Presenter" and who will be the "Questioner" first.

    - Explain that the roles will be switched after a set amount of time.

© Ahal Besorai 2023

3. **Presentation and Basic Questions (10-15 minutes)**
    - Ask the Presenters to share a personal issue or challenge they are currently facing with their partner.
    - Instruct the Questioners to ask only basic, unprocessed questions to explore the Presenter's perspective and gain a deeper understanding.
    - Encourage the Questioners to avoid assumptions, advice, or judgments in their questions.
    - Provide a list of examples for basic questions, such as:
        - "Can you tell me more about that?"
        - "What do you think caused this situation?"
        - "How does this challenge affect you?"
        - "What have you tried so far?"
        - "What support do you need right now?"

4. **Role Switch (5 minutes)**

© Ahal Besorai 2023

- After the allocated time, instruct the pairs to switch roles, with the Presenter becoming the Questioner and vice versa.
- Repeat steps 3 and 4, allowing the new Questioner to ask basic, unprocessed questions to explore the Presenter's perspective.

5. **Reflection and Discussion (5 minutes)**
   - Bring the participants back together as a group.
   - Facilitate a brief discussion by asking the following questions:
     - Presenters: How did it feel to have someone ask basic questions without offering advice or judgments?
     - Questioners: What challenges did you encounter in asking basic, unprocessed questions?
     - How did this exercise help you practice the beginner's mindset and active listening?

Closing:

- Thank all participants for their active engagement in the exercise and their commitment to asking basic, unprocessed questions.

- Highlight the importance of approaching personal issues with curiosity and open-mindedness.

- Encourage participants to incorporate the practice of asking basic questions into their everyday conversations, fostering deeper understanding and support.

Note: Adjust the duration of each phase based on the number of participants and the depth of discussion desired. Remind participants that the focus of the exercise is on asking basic, unprocessed questions rather than providing advice or judgments. Encourage them to embrace the beginner's mind, setting aside assumptions and approaching each conversation with curiosity and a genuine desire to understand.

Be creative.

Exercise: Role Play for 8 Participants

Duration: Approximately 60-90 minutes

Materials needed: Scenario descriptions, role assignment sheets, writing materials for participants, a timer (optional)

© Ahal Besorai 2023

Scenario: Rebuilding Trust in a Family (a different scenario may be chosen)

Description: You are a member of a closely-knit family that has experienced a significant breach of trust, resulting in strained relationships and a breakdown in communication. The incident has caused emotional pain and distance among family members. In an attempt to heal and rebuild trust, you have organized a role play exercise where each participant takes on a specific role to address the underlying issues and work towards reconciliation within the family.

Role Assignments:

1. Family Member A (You): The family member who feels betrayed and hurt, seeking understanding, acknowledgment, and a path towards forgiveness.

2. Family Member B: The family member responsible for the breach of trust, acknowledging the wrongdoing and expressing genuine remorse.

3. Family Member C: A neutral family member who acts as a mediator, encouraging open dialogue and facilitating the rebuilding of trust.

© Ahal Besorai 2023

4. Family Member D: The family member who has been affected by the incident but remains hesitant to trust again.

5. Family Member E: The optimist who holds hope for reconciliation and emphasizes the importance of forgiveness and moving forward.

6. Family Member F: The listener and supporter who provides a safe space for emotions to be expressed and encourages empathy among family members.

7. Family Member G: The sceptic who questions the possibility of rebuilding trust and remains cautious about the sincerity of the involved family members.

8. Observer: Takes notes during the role play and provides feedback on the dynamics, communication styles, and progress towards rebuilding trust.

Instructions:

1. *Introduction:*
    - Gather all participants and explain the purpose of the role play exercise.

- Describe the breach of trust situation within the family, emphasizing the goal of healing, understanding, and rebuilding trust.

- Stress the importance of active participation, empathy, and maintaining a non-judgmental attitude throughout the exercise.

2. *Role Assignment and Preparation:*

    - Provide each participant with their assigned role and a description of their character.

    - Allow participants 5 minutes to read their role descriptions, understand their motivations, perspectives, and potential actions within the scenario.

3. *Scenario Enactment:*

    - Set a timeframe of 30-45 minutes for the role play.

    - Initiate the role play, simulating a family gathering or meeting where the family members address the breach of trust and work towards rebuilding trust and understanding.

© Ahal Besorai 2023

- Encourage participants to fully embody their roles, engage in open and honest discussions, express their emotions authentically, and explore ways to rebuild trust within the family.

4. *Observer Feedback:*
    - Designate one or more participants as observers.
    - Instruct observers to take notes during the role play, focusing on effective strategies used, areas for improvement, and notable moments of progress or breakthroughs.
    - Allow observers 5 minutes to gather their thoughts and prepare feedback.

5. *Reflection and Debriefing:*
    - Conclude the role play and gather all participants for a group discussion.
    - Ask participants to share their experiences, thoughts, emotions, challenges faced, and lessons learned during the role play.
    - Encourage participants to reflect on the dynamics, interactions, and decisions made within the scenario.

© Ahal Besorai 2023

- Facilitate a debriefing discussion, exploring different perspectives, highlighting key takeaways, and discussing steps to rebuild trust and strengthen familial bonds.

6. *Optional: Iteration and Practice (if time permits):*
    - If time allows, repeat the role play with participants switching roles to explore different dynamics and strategies for rebuilding trust.
    - Follow steps 2-5 for the iteration, adjusting the timeframe as needed.

Closing:

- Thank all participants for their active involvement and willingness to engage in the role play exercise.
- Summarize the key insights and learnings from the discussion.
- Encourage participants to apply the lessons learned from the exercise.

Note: The suggested timeframe is approximate and can be adjusted based on the complexity of the scenario and the depth of discussion desired. Ensure that all participants have a chance to actively participate and share their thoughts during the reflection and debriefing phase.

Concrete Example: Role Play to Assist with a Deep Personal Issue

Scenario: John is a member of your Forum who updated that he's struggling with unresolved feelings of guilt and regret from a past event in his life. John decides to bring this deep personal issue to a Forum exploration to seek understanding, gain perspective, and explore potential paths towards healing and forgiveness.

Steps:

1. **Introduction:**
   - John shares his deep personal issue with the group, expressing his struggle with unresolved guilt and regret.
   - The group creates a safe and non-judgmental space, ensuring confidentiality and empathy for John's vulnerability.

2. **Role Assignment:**
   - The moderator assigns roles to different participants, considering key roles involved in

John's situation (e.g., John, a trusted friend, a family member, a therapist, an inner voice).

- Each participant is provided with a brief description of their role and any specific characteristics or behaviours they should portray.

3. **Role Play:**

    - John takes on his role and narrates the specific event or circumstance that has led to his feelings of guilt and regret.

    - Other participants embody their assigned roles and interact with John, providing support, asking probing questions, offering guidance, and representing different perspectives relevant to the issue.

4. **Reflection and Feedback:**

    - After the role play, John reflects on the experience and shares his emotional responses, insights gained, and any shifts in perspective.

    - Other participants provide compassionate feedback to John, sharing their observations, empathizing with his feelings, and offering alternative viewpoints or coping strategies.

5. **Iteration and Practice (optional):**

    o If time allows and the group feels it would be beneficial, the role play can be repeated with different scenarios or variations to further explore John's feelings, beliefs, and potential paths towards healing and forgiveness.

    o The roles and interactions can be adjusted based on the evolving dynamics and specific objectives.

6. **Group Discussion and Support:**

    o The group engages in an open and supportive discussion, allowing participants to share their personal experiences, insights, and lessons learned from similar situations.

    o Participants offer compassionate support, resources, and practical advice to help John navigate his journey towards healing and self-forgiveness.

7. **Action Planning:**

© Ahal Besorai 2023

- John formulates an action plan based on the collective wisdom and suggestions received during the role play and discussion.

- The group provides ongoing support and encouragement, assisting John in setting realistic goals, identifying potential therapeutic resources, or suggesting self-care practices.

Closing:

- The group concludes the session by expressing appreciation for John's willingness to share his deep personal issue and engage in the role play exercise.

- John expresses gratitude for the group's support, empathy, and insights, acknowledging the significance of the session in his journey towards healing.

- The group encourages continued communication, check-ins, and further exploration of the issue in future sessions, fostering a safe space for personal growth and support.

Through role play, John was able to explore his deep personal issue in a supportive and non-threatening environment. The exercise allowed him to gain insights, receive empathy and guidance from others, and develop a roadmap for addressing his unresolved guilt and regret. By engaging in this role play, John took an important step towards healing and finding a path towards forgiveness and self-acceptance.

© Ahal Besorai 2023

Openness

Openness is a personality trait that refers to being receptive to new ideas, experiences, and perspectives. While some people may naturally be more open-minded than others, research has shown that openness can also be cultivated through intentional effort and training. Here are some strategies that can help you train yourself to be more open:

1. Expose yourself to new experiences: Seek out new experiences, such as traveling to a new place, trying new foods, or learning a new skill. This can help you expand your perspective and challenge your assumptions.

2. Seek out diverse perspectives: Engage with people who have different perspectives and backgrounds than your own. This can help you see things from different angles and challenge your assumptions.

3. Practice active listening: When you engage in conversations with others, make an effort to really listen to what they are saying. Avoid interrupting or judging, and instead try to understand their perspective.

4. Practice empathy: Try to put yourself in other people's shoes and see things from their perspective. This can help you understand why they think and feel the way they do.

5. Challenge your assumptions: Be aware of your own biases and assumptions and make an effort to challenge them. This can help you see things from a fresh perspective and be more open-minded.

6. Keep an open mind: Finally, make a conscious effort to approach new experiences and ideas with an open mind. Avoid immediately dismissing things that seem unfamiliar or uncomfortable, and instead try to approach them with curiosity and a willingness to learn.

By practicing these strategies, you can gradually train yourself to be more open-minded and receptive to new ideas and experiences.

Openness Exercises

Exercise 1: Exploring Your Strong Opinions

Objective: To challenge and refine your perspectives by engaging with opposing viewpoints.

Time Needed: Approximately 30-45 minutes.

Materials Needed:

- Pen and paper or a digital note-taking device
- Internet access for research (optional)

Instructions:

Choose a Topic: Select a topic or subject that evokes a strong opinion within you. It could be related to politics, religion, ethics, or any other matter of personal significance.

State Your Opinion: Write down your opinion regarding the chosen topic. Clearly express your stance in a single sentence.

List Supporting Reasons: Identify and note down at least three reasons that support your opinion. These should be the main arguments that reinforce your viewpoint.

Identify Counterpoints: Deliberately seek out an opposing viewpoint or a piece of information that challenges your opinion. This could be an alternative perspective, contradictory data, or a differing personal experience.

Research the Opposing Viewpoint: If possible, spend some time researching and understanding the opposing viewpoint. Explore why some individuals hold this perspective and the rationale behind their beliefs.

© Ahal Besorai 2023

Reflect on Challenges: Take a moment to consider how this opposing viewpoint challenges your original opinion. Note down your initial reactions and thoughts.

Evaluate Impact: Assess how engaging with the opposing viewpoint has influenced your thinking. Has it altered your stance in any way? Do you find yourself more open to understanding different perspectives?

Summarize Learnings: Write a brief summary of your experience. Highlight any insights gained, whether your opinion evolved, and the value of considering differing viewpoints.

Note: The goal of this exercise isn't necessarily to change your opinion, but to foster critical thinking, empathy, and a broader understanding of complex issues.

Possible discussion topics

Climate Change: Explore your stance on climate change and its causes, effects, and solutions.

Gun Control: Delve into your opinions about gun control regulations and the Second Amendment.

Universal Healthcare: Reflect on your thoughts about universal healthcare versus privatized healthcare systems.

© Ahal Besorai 2023

Capital Punishment: Examine your perspective on the ethical and practical aspects of the death penalty.

Online Privacy: Consider your beliefs regarding online privacy, data collection, and surveillance.

Education System: Evaluate your opinions on the current education system, standardized testing, and alternative approaches.

Immigration Policies: Contemplate your stance on immigration laws, border control, and refugees.

Veganism vs. Carnivorism: Compare your viewpoints on adopting a vegan lifestyle versus consuming animal products.

Digital Currency: Explore your thoughts on the rise of digital currencies like Bitcoin and their potential impact on traditional economies.

Freedom of Speech: Examine your opinions about the boundaries and responsibilities of free speech in modern society.

Exercise 2: Embracing Novel Experiences

Objective: Expand your openness to new ideas, fostering personal growth and a more receptive mindset.

© Ahal Besorai 2023

Time Needed: Varies based on the activity but allocate at least 1 hour for the entire process.

Instructions:

1. **Choose a New Experience:** Select an activity or encounter that you've never tried before but find intriguing. This could range from sampling an unfamiliar cuisine to exploring a new skill or hobby.

2. **Embrace Curiosity:** Approach the chosen experience with a genuine sense of curiosity. Put aside any preconceived notions or expectations you might have.

3. **Engage Openly:** As you immerse yourself in the new activity, remain attuned to your thoughts and emotions. Notice any feelings of excitement, discomfort, or resistance that arise during the process.

4. **Capture Insights:** Throughout the experience, make a mental note of any fresh insights or perspectives you acquire. Reflect on how the encounter is shaping your understanding of yourself and the world.

5. **Reflect on Learnings:** After the activity, take time to reflect on how the experience influenced your thoughts and emotions. What did you discover about yourself or

the world? Did the encounter challenge your assumptions?

6. **Apply Lessons:** Consider how the insights from this exercise can extend to other facets of your life. How can you adopt a more open-minded stance when approaching future experiences or challenges?

Note: This exercise nurtures personal development by encouraging you to venture beyond your comfort zone and embrace novel experiences with an open heart and mind. Practicing this approach can lead to greater adaptability and personal growth. You can repeatedly undertake this exercise with various activities to continually nurture an open mindset.

Potential new experiences

Cook a New Recipe: Choose a dish from a cuisine you're not familiar with and attempt to cook it from scratch.

Learn a Musical Instrument: Begin learning to play a musical instrument you've never tried before.

Try a Different Art Form: Experiment with painting, sculpting, or any form of artistic expression that's new to you.

Attend a Workshop: Participate in a workshop on a topic you've never explored, such as mindfulness, pottery, or creative writing.

Visit a New Place: Travel to a nearby town or area you've never been to and explore its attractions.

Read Outside Your Comfort Zone: Choose a book from a genre or author you wouldn't typically read.

Engage in a Physical Activity: Try a fitness class or sport that you've never experienced before, like yoga, rock climbing, or dance.

Volunteer for a Cause: Dedicate time to volunteer for an organization or cause you're not familiar with.

Learn a New Language: Begin learning the basics of a language you've never studied.

Take up Gardening: Cultivate a garden with plants you've never grown before.

Attend a Cultural Event: Participate in a cultural festival, art exhibit, or performance that's new to you.

Try Meditation: Engage in meditation or mindfulness exercises to experience a different state of mind.

Spend Time in Nature: Explore a natural setting you've never visited, such as a forest, beach, or mountain trail.

Exercise 3: Navigating Diverse Perspectives

© Ahal Besorai 2023

Objective: Foster an open-minded and adaptable mindset by engaging in meaningful conversations with individuals who hold differing opinions.

Time Needed: Allocate around 1 hour for conversation and reflection.

Instructions:

1. **Select a Conversation Partner:** Choose someone you know, such as a friend, family member, or colleague, who holds opinions or beliefs that differ from your own.
2. **Schedule the Conversation:** Set aside dedicated time for the conversation. Inform your partner that you value their perspective and are eager to understand their point of view.
3. **Active Listening:** During the conversation, practice active listening. Allow your partner to express their opinions without interruption or judgment. Seek clarity by asking open-ended questions.
4. **Reflective Listening:** Engage in reflective listening by paraphrasing your partner's key points and repeating them back. This demonstrates your genuine interest in comprehending their standpoint.

© Ahal Besorai 2023

5. **Express Your Perspective:** Share your viewpoint in a respectful and non-confrontational manner. Focus on presenting your thoughts clearly without belittling their perspective.
6. **Find Common Ground:** Look for areas of agreement or shared values. While complete agreement might not always be possible, identifying common ground can foster mutual respect and understanding.
7. **Reflect on the Experience:** After the conversation, take time to reflect on what you've learned and how the dialogue influenced your understanding of their viewpoint and your own.

Note: This exercise enhances your communication skills, empathy, and adaptability. Regularly engaging in conversations with diverse perspectives nurtures open-mindedness, enriches your perspective, and contributes to more meaningful interactions.

Exercise 4: Topic: Building Openness

Time: 30-45 minutes

Materials: Blank paper, pens, a timer

Number of participants: 8-10

Instructions:

1. Explain to the group that they will be engaging in a reflection and discussion exercise on the topic of openness. Encourage them to approach the exercise with an open and curious mindset.

2. Ask each participant to take a few minutes to reflect on a time when they felt closed-minded or resistant to new ideas or perspectives. Encourage them to write down their thoughts and feelings on the situation.

3. After everyone has had a chance to reflect, divide the group into pairs. Ask each pair to share their reflection with their partner, and to listen actively to their partner's story.

4. After a set period of time, ask each person to switch partners and share their reflection with a new partner. Encourage partners to ask questions and to provide feedback or support as needed.

5. After everyone has had a chance to share their reflection with multiple partners, reconvene the group as a whole. Ask for volunteers to share their reflections with the larger group, summarizing what they learned about themselves and their approach to openness.

© Ahal Besorai 2023

6. As a group, discuss the reflections and any common themes or challenges that emerged. Encourage participants to share strategies they use to cultivate openness and curiosity, and to brainstorm ways the group can support each other in this effort.

By engaging in this exercise, group members can reflect on their own approach to openness and cultivate a deeper understanding of the challenges and benefits of approaching new ideas and perspectives with an open mindset. The exercise also promotes active listening and discussion among group members.

Ritual

1. Find a quiet and peaceful place where you won't be disturbed. This could be a room in your home, a park, or any other location where you feel comfortable and relaxed.

2. Sit or stand comfortably, with your eyes closed or softly focused.

3. Take a few deep breaths and focus on your breathing. Try to clear your mind of any distractions or worries.

4. Visualize a symbol or image that represents openness to you. This could be an open door, a butterfly, or any other image that resonates with you.

5. Hold this image in your mind and focus on the feelings of openness and curiosity that it represents. Allow yourself to feel a sense of openness and receptivity to new experiences, ideas, and perspectives.

6. Repeat a simple mantra or affirmation to reinforce your commitment to openness. For example, you could repeat to yourself, "I'm open to new experiences and ideas" or "I approach the world with curiosity and openness."

7. Take a few more deep breaths, and then slowly open your eyes.

You can repeat this ritual daily or whenever you feel the need to cultivate a greater sense of openness and curiosity. By regularly focusing your attention on openness and committing to a mindset of curiosity and receptivity, you can begin to cultivate a more open-minded approach to the world around you.

Curiosity

Curiosity can be defined as a strong desire to learn or know something by being inquisitive, asking questions, and exploring new ideas. It's a natural human inclination to seek new information and experiences, and to try to make sense of the world around us.

In the context of a YPO Forum, curiosity can play an important role in fostering innovation, growth, and learning. YPO is a community of leaders who are constantly seeking new ideas, insights, and strategies to improve their businesses and organizations. By encouraging curiosity and creating opportunities for members to explore new ideas and perspectives, YPO can help its members stay ahead of the curve, adapt to change, and stay competitive in their respective industries.

Curiosity can also help YPO members build stronger relationships and networks. By asking questions and showing a genuine interest in other members' experiences and perspectives, YPO members can build deeper connections and find new opportunities for collaboration and partnership.

Overall, curiosity is an essential trait for YPO members to cultivate as they navigate the complex and ever-changing

© Ahal Besorai 2023

landscape of business and leadership. It allows them to stay open to new ideas and perspectives, adapt to change, and continue to grow and learn as individuals and leaders.

Exercise: Embracing Curiosity through Exploration

Objective: Cultivate curiosity and openness by immersing yourself in unfamiliar activities, embracing discomfort, and learning from new experiences.

Time Needed: Allocate approximately 1-2 hours for the activity and reflection.

Instructions:

1. **Choose an Unfamiliar Activity**: Set aside dedicated time to engage in an activity that you have little to no familiarity with. This could be trying a new cuisine, listening to a different genre of music, or attempting a creative hobby.

2. **Monitor Thoughts and Emotions**: As you participate in the activity, be mindful of any resistance, discomfort, or curiosity that arises. Observe your emotional responses without judgment.

3. **Embrace Discomfort Mindfully**: Practice accepting any discomfort that surfaces during the experience.

Allow yourself to acknowledge and feel the emotions without attempting to suppress or avoid them.

4. **Approach with Curiosity**: Engage in the activity with a sense of curiosity and openness. Approach it as if you were a beginner, devoid of preconceived notions or expectations.

5. **Reflect on the Experience**: After the activity, take time to reflect on what you learned from engaging in this new experience. Did your feelings or thoughts change as you became more familiar with the activity?

Note: Regularly participating in this exercise nurtures a mindset of openness to novel experiences and viewpoints. It also develops resilience in the face of discomfort or uncertainty, aiding in your comfort with the unknown.

Group Variation: Curiosity Exploration

Objective: Foster group curiosity and understanding by researching and sharing topics of interest.

Time Needed: Approximately 1-2 hours, depending on group size and discussion depth.

Instructions:

© Ahal Besorai 2023

1. **Choose Curiosity Topics**: Have each member of the group select a topic they're curious about, whether it's a new technology, a hobby, or a cultural practice.

2. **Share Topic Choices**: In a round-robin manner, each member explains their chosen topic to the group, highlighting what intrigues them about it.

3. **Form Research Subgroups**: Divide the group into smaller subgroups of two members each. Assign each subgroup the task of thoroughly researching one member's chosen topic.

4. **Research Deeply**: Encourage each subgroup to explore their assigned topic in detail, gathering information from various sources and perspectives.

5. **Presentation and Discussion**: After a designated time, reconvene as a full group. Each subgroup presents their findings, sharing different viewpoints and insights they uncovered.

6. **Group Discussion**: Engage in a collective discussion about the diverse perspectives and newfound knowledge gained through the research process.

Note: This group activity fosters a collaborative approach to curiosity, encouraging participants to explore unfamiliar topics and learn from each other's research. The discussion promotes open-mindedness and expands understanding within the group.

Exercise: Fostering Curiosity

By engaging in this exercise, group members can develop a sense of curiosity about a variety of topics and can learn to approach new information with an open and inquisitive mind. The exercise also promotes collaboration and the sharing of knowledge and ideas among group members.

Topic: Cultivating Curiosity

Time: 30-45 minutes

Materials: Blank paper, pens, a timer

Number of participants: 8-10

Instructions:

1. Explain to the group that they will be engaging in a rapid-fire questioning exercise. Each person will have one minute to ask as many questions as they can about a specific topic.

2. Assign a different topic to each person in the group. The topics can be anything from current events to personal interests. Encourage participants to choose a

topic that they are curious about and want to learn more about.

3. Set a timer for one minute and have the first person in the group start asking questions about their topic. The other members of the group can answer the questions or provide additional information, if they have it.

4. After one minute, have the next person in the group take their turn asking questions about their assigned topic. Repeat this process until every member of the group has had a chance to ask questions.

5. After the exercise, have the group reflect on the experience. Ask questions such as: What did you learn through this exercise? Did you discover anything new or surprising about your topic or your group members? How did it feel to ask questions in this rapid-fire format?

By engaging in this exercise, group members can practice their curiosity skills and learn to approach new information with an open and inquisitive mind. The exercise also promotes active listening and the sharing of knowledge and perspectives among group members.

Ritual

1. Take a walk in a familiar environment, such as your neighbourhood or a nearby park.

2. Choose a specific focus for your walk, such as observing the different types of trees or noticing the different architectural styles of the houses in your neighbourhood.

3. As you walk, pay close attention to your surroundings and notice details that you might have overlooked before.

4. Use your senses to explore your environment. Touch the bark of a tree, listen to the sound of birds chirping, or smell the flowers in a nearby garden.

5. Ask yourself questions about what you are observing. Why do certain houses have unique architectural styles? What kind of trees are common in your area and what are their benefits to the ecosystem?

6. Reflect on your experience and what you have learned. Did you discover anything new or surprising? How can you use this knowledge to deepen your connection to your environment and community?

By approaching your everyday surroundings with curiosity and a sense of wonder, you can cultivate a deeper appreciation for the world around you and develop a greater understanding of the natural and built environments in which you live.

© Ahal Besorai 2023

Authenticity

Authenticity refers to being true to oneself and acting in accordance with one's values, beliefs, and personality. It involves being honest with oneself and others, and not pretending to be someone you aren't. Authenticity is important because it leads to a greater sense of self-awareness, self-acceptance, and self-expression, which can lead to greater happiness and fulfilment in life.

In the context of a YPO Forum, authenticity is relevant because it creates a culture of openness, trust, and respect among members. When members are authentic, they are able to share their true thoughts and feelings, which promotes more meaningful and productive discussions. Authenticity also encourages members to be vulnerable, which can lead to deeper connections and more authentic relationships.

Additionally, authenticity can help members navigate difficult situations and conflicts within the Forum. When members are authentic, they are more likely to express their concerns and needs in a constructive way, which can help to resolve conflicts in a positive and productive manner. Overall, authenticity is an important value to promote within a YPO Forum to create a supportive and productive community.

© Ahal Besorai 2023

Exercise: Exploring Authenticity

Time: 30-45 minutes

Materials: Blank paper, pens, a timer

Number of participants: 8-10

Instructions:

1. Explain to the group that they will be engaging in an exercise designed to explore authenticity. Encourage them to approach the exercise with an open and curious mindset.

2. Ask each participant to take a few minutes to reflect on a time when they felt they were not being authentic. Encourage them to write down their thoughts and feelings on the situation.

3. After everyone has had a chance to reflect, ask each person to share their reflection with the group. Encourage them to be as open and honest as possible in their sharing.

4. After each person has had a chance to share, ask for volunteers to share any common themes or challenges that emerged from the reflections.

© Ahal Besorai 2023

5. As a group, discuss the reflections and any strategies that can be used to cultivate authenticity. Encourage participants to share their own experiences with being authentic and any tips they have for staying true to oneself.

6. As a final step, ask each person to identify one action they can take in the coming week to be more authentic in their personal or professional life. Encourage them to write down this action and to share it with the group if they feel comfortable.

By engaging in this exercise, group members can explore their own approach to authenticity and gain insights into the challenges and benefits of being true to oneself. The exercise also promotes open and honest discussion among group members, as well as practical strategies for cultivating authenticity.

Exercise: Authenticity in Action

Time: 60-75 minutes

Materials: Flipchart or whiteboard, markers, sticky notes, pens

Number of participants: 8-10

Objective: To encourage participants to practice authenticity in real-life scenarios and gain firsthand experience in authentic communication.

Instructions:

1. Introduction (5 minutes): Start by explaining the importance of authenticity in communication and how it can lead to stronger relationships and better outcomes in both personal and professional settings.
2. Scenario Selection (10 minutes): Prepare a list of common scenarios that involve communication (e.g., a job interview, a disagreement with a colleague, giving and receiving feedback, or a personal relationship conversation). Write each scenario on a separate sticky note.
3. Scenario Distribution (5 minutes): Place the sticky notes face down on a table or display them on a wall. Ask each participant to pick one sticky note without revealing its content.
4. Scenario Reflection (10 minutes): Give participants time to read the scenario on their chosen sticky note. Ask them to reflect individually on how they would typically approach this scenario, considering their

© Ahal Besorai 2023

usual communication style and whether it aligns with their authentic self.

5. Authentic Response Plan (15 minutes): Encourage participants to plan how they would approach the scenario authentically. What words would they use? What tone? What non-verbal cues? Emphasize that authenticity doesn't mean being blunt or unfiltered but rather being true to one's values, feelings, and intentions.

6. Role-Playing (20 minutes): Pair participants randomly and have them take turns role-playing the scenario they selected. One person plays the role of themselves, striving to communicate authentically based on their plan. The other person plays the role of the other party in the scenario.

7. Feedback and Discussion (15 minutes): After each role-play, invite the pairs to provide constructive feedback to each other. Encourage them to share what felt authentic and effective in the communication and what could be improved.

8. Group Discussion (10 minutes): Lead a group discussion where participants share their experiences from the role-plays. Discuss any challenges they faced in being authentic and any breakthrough moments they

experienced. Encourage the group to offer insights and suggestions for improving authenticity in communication.

9. Action Commitment (10 minutes): Ask each participant to choose one specific action they will take in their daily life to communicate more authentically based on what they've learned during the exercise. Have them write this commitment on a piece of paper or a sticky note.

10. Closing Remarks (5 minutes): Conclude the exercise by emphasizing the value of authentic communication and encouraging participants to practice their chosen actions in real-life situations.

This exercise allows participants to actively practice authenticity in various scenarios, receive feedback, and learn from each other's experiences. It promotes self-awareness and provides practical tools for improving authentic communication skills.

Exercise: Authenticity Reflection

Time: 30-45 minutes

Materials: Blank paper, pens

Number of participants: 8-10

Instructions:

© Ahal Besorai 2023

1. Introduce the topic of authenticity and explain that the purpose of this exercise is to reflect on what authenticity means to each participant.

2. Ask each participant to take a few minutes to reflect on and write down their personal definition of authenticity. Encourage them to be as specific and detailed as possible.

3. Once everyone has finished writing, have each person share their definition with the group. Encourage the group to discuss any commonalities or differences in their definitions.

4. Next, ask each person to reflect on a time in their life when they felt their most authentic. Encourage them to write down as much detail as possible about the situation, their thoughts, and their feelings.

5. After everyone has had time to reflect and write, have each person share their experience with the group. Encourage the group to discuss any commonalities or differences in their experiences.

6. Finally, ask each person to identify one action they can take in the next week to increase their authenticity in their daily life. Encourage them to write this action

down and to share it with the group if they feel comfortable.

By engaging in this exercise, group members can reflect on their personal definition of authenticity, share their experiences of authenticity, and identify practical strategies for increasing authenticity in their daily lives. The exercise promotes open and honest discussion among group members and encourages the development of practical strategies for living more authentically.

Ritual: Authenticity Visualization Ritual

Time: 10-15 minutes

Materials: A quiet, comfortable space

Instructions:

1. Find a quiet, comfortable space where you won't be interrupted for 10-15 minutes.
2. Begin by taking a few deep breaths and allowing yourself to relax.
3. Close your eyes and visualize yourself in a situation where you feel completely authentic. This could be a past experience or a future scenario.

© Ahal Besorai 2023

4. Imagine yourself fully embracing your authentic self in this situation. Picture yourself speaking and acting in alignment with your true self.

5. Take note of how you feel in this moment of complete authenticity. What emotions are present? What thoughts are going through your mind?

6. After a few minutes of visualization, slowly bring yourself back to the present moment.

7. Take a few moments to journal about your experience. Write down any insights or reflections that came to mind during the visualization.

By engaging in this visualization ritual, you can focus on the experience of being authentic and identify what it feels like to fully embrace your true self. The ritual encourages self-awareness and mindfulness and helps to promote a sense of connection with your authentic self.

© Ahal Besorai 2023

Respect

Respect is a term that refers to a positive feeling or action shown towards someone or something that is considered important or valuable. It's about recognizing the inherent worth and dignity of others, treating them with consideration, and refraining from actions that would harm or diminish their well-being.

In the context of a YPO Forum, respect is essential for building and maintaining positive relationships among members. It allows for open and honest communication, even in the face of disagreement or differing opinions. When members feel respected, they are more likely to share their thoughts and ideas without fear of judgment or criticism. This can lead to greater innovation and progress within the group.

Respect also helps to create a culture of inclusivity and diversity. When members feel valued and respected regardless of their background, beliefs, or experiences, it can promote a sense of belonging and unity within the group. This can lead to greater collaboration and cooperation, as members work towards common goals and objectives.

© Ahal Besorai 2023

Overall, fostering respect within a YPO Forum is essential for creating a positive and productive environment where members can thrive both personally and professionally.

Respect is a fundamental value that involves treating others with consideration, dignity, and kindness. It's about acknowledging the worth and individuality of each person, regardless of their background, beliefs, or opinions. Respecting others means being mindful of their boundaries, being courteous and polite, and refraining from judgment or discrimination.

Exercise: Respect Mapping

Time: 30-45 minutes

Materials: Large sheets of paper, markers

Instructions:

1. Divide participants into pairs.
2. Ask each pair to take a large sheet of paper and draw a mind-map of what respect looks like to them. Encourage them to be creative and use symbols, words, and images to represent different aspects of respect.

© Ahal Besorai 2023

3. Once each pair has completed their map, bring the group back together and ask them to share their maps with one another.

4. Encourage participants to ask questions and seek clarification about the different symbols and images on each map.

5. After everyone has had a chance to share their map, ask the group to identify common themes and patterns across the different maps.

6. Ask participants to reflect on what they learned about respect through this exercise and how they can apply these lessons to their daily lives.

By engaging in this exercise, participants have the opportunity to explore their own understanding of respect and learn from the perspectives of others. The exercise encourages creativity and collaboration and helps to promote a sense of shared understanding and respect.

Exercise: Respect Role Play

Time: 30-45 minutes

Materials: None

Instructions:

1. Divide the participants into pairs.

2. Ask each pair to take turns role-playing a scenario in which one person is showing disrespect towards the other. For example, one person might be speaking over the other, interrupting them, or using a derogatory term.

3. After each role-play, ask the other participant to share how they felt during the interaction and what they would have preferred to happen instead.

4. Encourage participants to switch roles and try the scenario again, this time incorporating the feedback from their partner.

5. Once everyone has had a chance to participate in the role-play, bring the group back together for a debrief. Ask the participants to reflect on what they learned about respect and how they can apply these lessons to their daily lives.

By engaging in this role-play exercise, participants have the opportunity to practice showing respect and responding to disrespect in a safe and controlled environment. The exercise encourages empathy and perspective-taking and helps to promote a sense of mutual understanding and respect.

© Ahal Besorai 2023

Exercise: Respect Walk

Time: 30-45 minutes

Materials: None

Instructions:

1. Divide participants into small groups of 3-4 people.

2. Ask each group to take a walk around an outside space.

3. As they walk, ask them to observe the environment around them and look for signs of respect or disrespect. For example, they might notice someone holding the door open for another person, or someone cutting in front of another person in a line.

4. Encourage participants to discuss their observations with one another and reflect on how they would feel if they were on the receiving end of those behaviours.

5. Once everyone has had a chance to share their observations and reflections, bring the group back together for a debrief.

6. Ask participants to share their key takeaways from the exercise and how they can apply these lessons to their daily lives.

© Ahal Besorai 2023

By engaging in this exercise, participants have the opportunity to observe and reflect on examples of respect and disrespect in their daily lives. The exercise encourages empathy and perspective-taking and helps to promote a sense of awareness and intentionality around respectful behaviours.

Action-oriented

Being action-oriented means having a mindset and approach that emphasizes taking action and getting things done. In the context of a YPO Forum, this can manifest in a few different ways. Firstly, it can mean setting clear goals and objectives for the group and then taking concrete steps towards achieving them. This might involve breaking down larger goals into smaller, more manageable tasks, assigning responsibilities and deadlines, and regularly checking in on progress.

Additionally, being action-oriented can mean actively seeking out opportunities for growth and development, both personally and as a group. This might involve identifying areas where the group could improve, such as in communication or leadership, and then taking steps to address those areas through training, workshops, or other forms of education.

Finally, being action-oriented means being willing to take calculated risks and make decisions, even in the face of uncertainty or ambiguity. This can involve being comfortable with experimentation and failure, as long as there is a willingness to learn from mistakes and adapt.

© Ahal Besorai 2023

Overall, being action-oriented is an important mindset to cultivate in a YPO Forum, as it can help drive progress and growth, both individually and collectively. By taking proactive steps towards goals and continuously seeking out opportunities for improvement, YPO members can stay motivated, engaged, and focused on achieving success.

As an executive coach and leadership development expert, I firmly believe that being action-oriented is a critical component of successful leadership. To be an effective leader, one must have the drive and initiative to take action and make things happen.

In the context of a YPO Forum, being action-oriented can help members move beyond simply discussing ideas and actually implement them. By taking action on the insights gained from Forum discussions, members can make real progress and drive meaningful change in their businesses and communities.

To cultivate a culture of action-orientedness within a YPO Forum, members must prioritize action and hold each other accountable for following through on commitments. This can be achieved through regular check-ins and progress updates, as well as by celebrating and recognizing those who demonstrate a commitment to action.

© Ahal Besorai 2023

Exercise: Action-Oriented Mindset Challenge

Time: 30-45 minutes

Materials: None

Instructions:

1. Divide the participants into small groups of 4-6 members each or do it with the whole Forum.

2. Provide each group with a hypothetical scenario* or challenge that requires prompt action and decision-making. It could be a business-related situation, a personal development challenge, or a community problem that needs to be addressed.

3. Instruct each group to brainstorm and discuss potential actions they would take to address the given scenario. Encourage them to think creatively and consider both individual and collaborative actions.

4. Set a specific time limit (e.g., 15-20 minutes) for the group to generate a list of actionable steps they would take in response to the scenario.

5. After the time limit, ask each group to present their action plans to the rest of the participants. Encourage

© Ahal Besorai 2023

them to share their ideas, strategies, and the rationale behind their chosen actions.

6. Facilitate a discussion among the groups, focusing on the following questions:

    - What were the common elements in the action plans developed by different groups?
    - How did the exercise challenge the participants to think more proactively and take action?
    - Did any group come up with particularly innovative or unique actions? If so, what made those actions stand out?

7. Summarize the key insights and strategies shared by the groups, emphasizing the importance of an action-oriented mindset and the value of taking proactive steps to overcome challenges and achieve desired outcomes.

8. Conclude the exercise with a reflection session where participants share their personal takeaways from the activity and discuss how they can apply the action-oriented mindset in their daily lives and professional pursuits.

© Ahal Besorai 2023

By engaging in this exercise, participants will actively explore and develop an action-oriented mindset, allowing them to approach challenges and opportunities with a proactive mindset and a bias towards taking action.

* Scenario 1: Business Expansion Dilemma You are the CEO of a small technology startup that has been growing rapidly. You are faced with the decision of whether to expand your business operations to a new market. The challenge is to identify the potential risks, opportunities, and steps needed to successfully enter the new market while ensuring continued growth and profitability.

Scenario 2: Personal Development Goal - Imagine you are an individual who wants to develop a new skill or pursue a personal goal. For example, you might have a desire to learn a musical instrument or improve your public speaking abilities. The challenge is to identify actionable steps and strategies that you can take to make progress towards your personal development goal, considering factors such as time commitment, resources needed, and potential obstacles to overcome.

Scenario 3: Environmental Sustainability Initiative - You are a member of an environmental organization aiming to promote sustainable practices in your community. The challenge is to

© Ahal Besorai 2023

develop an initiative that raises awareness about environmental issues and encourages sustainable behaviours. Your task is to brainstorm actionable steps and strategies to implement the initiative, including outreach activities, educational campaigns, and partnerships with local stakeholders.

Exercise: Action-Oriented Member Sharing Circle

Time: 30-45 minutes

Materials: None

Instructions:

1. Gather all members in a circle or seating arrangement that allows for open communication and engagement.

2. Explain the objective of the exercise, which is to cultivate an action-oriented attitude in member sharing.

3. Set the ground rules for the sharing circle, emphasizing active listening, respect, and confidentiality.

4. Select a facilitator who will guide the process and ensure everyone has an opportunity to share.

5. The facilitator starts by sharing a personal challenge, opportunity, or goal they have been facing. They

© Ahal Besorai 2023

should provide sufficient context and details to help others understand the situation.

6. After sharing their own experience, the facilitator explicitly states what kind of action-oriented response or support they are seeking from the group. For example, they may ask for practical suggestions, resources, or accountability.

7. The facilitator then invites the next person in the circle to share their own challenge, opportunity, or goal. Encourage each member to take turns sharing and seeking action-oriented responses from the group.

8. As each person shares, the other members actively listen and engage in a discussion, offering their insights, experiences, or suggestions on how the individual can take concrete steps towards their desired outcome.

9. Encourage members to ask clarifying questions, provide encouragement, and challenge each other to think in terms of actionable solutions.

10. Ensure that each member receives adequate time and attention for their sharing and discussion.

© Ahal Besorai 2023

11. Conclude the exercise by reflecting on the experience as a group. Discuss the benefits of an action-oriented attitude in member sharing and how it can empower individuals to take proactive steps in addressing their challenges or pursuing their goals.

12. Encourage participants to carry the action-oriented mindset into their daily interactions and support each other in taking tangible actions towards their personal and professional aspirations.

By engaging in this exercise, members will have the opportunity to share their challenges, goals, and opportunities within a supportive and action-oriented environment. The exercise encourages active listening, collaboration, and the exchange of practical ideas, empowering individuals to take concrete steps towards their desired outcomes.

Exercise: Collaborative Vision Board Creation

Time: 45-60 minutes

Materials: Magazines, scissors, glue sticks, large poster boards or flipchart paper, markers, colored pencils

Number of participants: 8-10

Objective: To encourage participants to visualize their personal or group goals, aspirations, and values, and collaboratively create a vision board that represents their shared vision.

Instructions:

1. Introduction (5 minutes): Begin by explaining the purpose of the exercise, which is to collectively create a vision board that reflects the group's shared goals, aspirations, and values.
2. Individual Reflection (10 minutes): Provide each participant with a stack of magazines, scissors, and glue sticks. Ask them to spend a few minutes flipping through the magazines and cutting out images, words, or phrases that resonate with their personal goals and aspirations. These can be related to their personal lives, careers, or any other relevant areas.
3. Group Vision Discussion (10 minutes): Divide the participants into small groups of 3-4 people each. In their small groups, encourage them to share the images, words, or phrases they have chosen and discuss what they represent for them individually. Encourage active listening and respect for each participant's vision.

© Ahal Besorai 2023

4. Collaborative Vision Board (15 minutes): Provide each small group with a large poster board or flipchart paper and markers. Instruct them to collaboratively arrange the images, words, and phrases they have selected onto the poster board, creating a shared vision board. Encourage them to arrange the elements creatively and meaningfully.
5. Group Sharing (10 minutes): After the small groups have created their vision boards, ask each group to present their board to the larger group. Have them explain the collective meaning behind the images and words they've chosen. Encourage open discussion and questions from the larger group.
6. Reflection and Synthesis (5 minutes): As a group, reflect on the common themes and values that have emerged from the individual vision boards. Discuss any shared aspirations and goals that have become apparent during the exercise.
7. Shared Vision Board (10 minutes): Now, combine the individual small group vision boards to create one large, shared vision board for the entire group. This board should represent the collective vision and aspirations of the entire group.

© Ahal Besorai 2023

8. Action Commitments (5 minutes): Conclude the exercise by having each participant commit to one actionable step they can take to contribute to the realization of the shared vision. Ask them to write down this commitment on a sticky note or piece of paper.
9. Group Discussion (5 minutes): Encourage participants to briefly share their individual action commitments with the group, fostering a sense of accountability and collaboration.

This exercise promotes shared goal setting, collaboration, and alignment of values within a group. It allows participants to create a tangible representation of their collective vision, which can serve as a source of inspiration and motivation for future endeavors. It also encourages meaningful conversations about personal aspirations and how they align with the group's vision.

Ritual: Procrastination-Busting Power Hour

Time: 1 hour

Instructions:

1. Find a quiet and comfortable space in your home where you can focus without distractions.

2. Set aside a dedicated hour each day for your Procrastination-Busting Power Hour.

3. Before you begin, make a list of tasks or projects that you have been procrastinating on. Write them down in a visible place.

4. Begin the Power Hour by setting a timer for 25 minutes. This will be your focused work interval.

5. Choose one task from your list and commit to working on it with full concentration for the entire 25 minutes.

6. During this focused work interval, eliminate distractions such as social media, phone notifications, or any other temptations that may lead to procrastination.

7. Engage in the task with a sense of urgency and purpose, reminding yourself of the benefits of completing it.

8. Once the 25 minutes are up, take a 5-minute break. Use this time to stretch, relax, or do something enjoyable.

9. After the break, set the timer for another 25-minute work interval and choose a different task from your list.

© Ahal Besorai 2023

10. If you complete a task during one work interval, celebrate your accomplishment and choose another task to work on for the next interval.

11. At the end of the Power Hour, take a few minutes to reflect on your progress. Acknowledge the tasks you completed and the progress you made in combating procrastination.

12. Carry over any unfinished tasks to the next Power Hour session or schedule dedicated time in the future to tackle them.

By implementing this Procrastination-Busting Power Hour ritual, you create dedicated time for focused work and break the cycle of procrastination. The structured intervals and breaks help maintain momentum and prevent burnout. With consistent practice, this ritual can help you develop a proactive and action-oriented approach to overcoming procrastination in your daily life.

© Ahal Besorai 2023